HALF A WIFE

Gaby Hinsliff started her career in 1994 as a reporter on the Grimsby *Evening Telegraph*, and within a decade had worked her way up to being Political Editor of the *Observer*. In 2007, she took nine months off after the birth of her son before going back to her old full-time job, but two years later she finally decided she'd had enough of life getting lost in the rush. The piece she wrote about this in the *Observer* was a sensation and prompted both her blog Used To Be Somebody and this book. She now lives and works – happily – with her husband and son in Oxfordshire.

Half a Wife

Gaby Hinsliff

Chatto & Windus
LONDON

Published by Chatto & Windus 2012

2 4 6 8 10 9 7 5 3 1

First published in Great Britain in 2012 by
Chatto & Windus
Random House, 20 Vauxhall Bridge Road,
London SW1V 2SA
www.randomhouse.co.uk

Addresses for companies within The Random House Group Limited can be found at:
www.randomhouse.co.uk/offices.htm

The Random House Group Limited Reg. No. 954009

A CIP catalogue record for this book
is available from the British Library

ISBN 9780701185985

The Random House Group Limited supports The Forest Stewardship Council
(FSC®), the leading international forest certification organisation. Our books
carrying the FSC label are printed on FSC® certified paper. FSC is the only forest
certification scheme endorsed by the leading environmental organisations, including
Greenpeace. Our paper procurement policy can be found at
www.randomhouse.co.uk/environment

Typeset in Baskerville MT by Palimpsest Book Production Limited,
Falkirk, Stirlingshire

Printed and bound in Great Britain by
Clays Ltd, St Ives plc

For Freddie: as everything usually is

CONTENTS

PROLOGUE

There is a concept in architecture known as a line of desire, and it means the route people take through public space that was never imagined on the architect's drawing. It might be the pretty, but winding, path through the trees; or it might be the illicit short cut, the rat run trampled across the lawn when the concrete path was supposed to lead people obediently around the edge. But either way it's really a sign of flawed design, because it means the space is not working quite in harmony with the way people actually want to use it.

There is just such a line of desire in British working life now, increasingly well trodden by parents turning their backs on the narrow old corporate career path. It's a line I followed myself just over two years ago, when I gave up a job I loved in order to take back the life it seemed to have cost me. And it's a line people often unthinkingly assume leads back home: but closer inspection reveals it's a lot more complicated, and rather less cosy, than that.

I have been professionally interested in family policy – the way the state influences and dictates parents' and employers' choices, the way economic circumstances sculpt intimate relationships, and vice versa – for nearly a decade longer than I have been a parent. It was clear to me from early on in my journalistic career that most of us experience and understand economic change first within the family: shocks are absorbed, dry statistical trends made flesh, shifts in spending become suddenly real to most of us only when they reach close to home. The political, you might say, is ultimately personal. But stupidly, none of that prepared me for having a baby.

Once upon a time, I interviewed prime ministers and travelled to war zones. As the political editor of a national newspaper, I spent 18-hour days happily absorbed in poking around beneath the government's skin. And when I got pregnant, at first it seemed as if nothing would change. Even when I could hardly reach the keyboard over my bump, I was still sometimes working until 3 a.m., and I never seriously considered giving up. When my son was born, I took nine months off, and was as excited as I was faintly terrified about going back to work.

My son seemed happy and thriving with our new nanny. But to my surprise I was the one who failed to settle, tormented by the secret running tally I kept in my head of how few hours a week he spent with his parents versus how many he spent being raised by someone else. And while my job had always been demanding, combining it with motherhood seemed to create a monster. The sheer amount of time sucked up by work plus baby squeezed out everything else but sleep, and often that too: I felt boxed in, flattened out, desperate to escape but ashamed of my desire to do so. Other people managed, didn't they? It was only when I stopped pretending everything was fine that I realised how many men and women I knew in dual career families were pretending too.

It would make for a neater story if I could explain exactly what tipped me over the edge. There are plenty of publicly acceptable stories I can reel off, of course: the time I broke up a family holiday early, to go home and deal with a Cabinet resignation, say. Or all those mornings my baby son woke bright-eyed at 5.30 a.m. and I crawled out of bed, almost hallucinating with tiredness after finishing work three hours before, desperate not to waste time with him. Or even the night before a work trip to Afghanistan, something I'd done without blinking in the past, when I lay awake for hours trying and failing to compose a letter for my little boy to read should the RAF flight somehow be shot down. (I gave up when I couldn't see for crying, and settled for a list explaining which of the already purchased family Christmas presents were intended for whom, obviously *the* burning issue in the event of my unlikely death.) But to me, none of these stories quite explain why I resigned a little less than two years after returning from maternity leave. The peculiar force of gravity that draws working parents back towards the home is often taken for granted; yet when it came for me, I was surprised by how little I understood it.

This book was conceived at least in part to explain to myself what on earth I had done. What follows is inevitably in some senses a memoir, a retracing of my own steps, and in writing it I have had to face some awkward truths about my mothering, my career and my marriage. Things are rarely as simple as we wish them to be. So I hope it will serve too as a loose kind of manual for those considering the same leap into the dark, and keen to avoid making some of my more obvious mistakes. But it is also in large part a manifesto, setting out changes both big and small that could create the time and space working parents need. For I never actually stopped working, although now it's more like three days a week instead of anywhere up to six; and I now work on many more projects – a wide variety of journalism, this book, a blog, broadcasting, policy analysis – than I would ever have had the chance to try had I stuck to that narrow conventional path.

For all the shifts in working life over the last couple of decades, the ideal career track for ambitious professionals remains broadly unchanged from their parents' day: a relentless upward trajectory through ever-rising levels of responsibility, rung by logical rung. It's the pure linear path of someone who doesn't have children or is happy to behave as if they didn't, with no changing priorities, hard-to-explain gaps or overwhelming desire to veer off sideways for a while. It's often referred to as a male career path, reflecting a common and erroneous assumption that only women's lives are changed by having children. But the trouble is that fathers are now beginning to rebel against it too.

And I think that's because it is really a sole breadwinner path, rather than somehow a biologically 'male' path. Working like this is fine if you have no domestic ties, or else a spouse at home taking care of the rest of your life – the raising of children, the running of a house, the nurturing of friends and loved ones, the time-consuming creation of a happy and richly rounded existence. But sole breadwinners are now an endangered species. The majority of couples with children both work, although one might be part-time, and it's the rise of these dual career families that has changed not just the face of modern parenting but of the modern workforce.

Three decades ago, the model of male breadwinner and female homemaker was the norm in British family life: in 1983, only one in five mothers of children under three went out to work.[1] But that picture is now almost completely reversed: by 2010, two-thirds of mothers were working.[2] By the time their children are safely off to primary school, around three in four couples are dual earners – and once the children are in secondary school, it's six out of seven couples.[3] Over half of mothers who work do so part-time, but there has nonetheless been a rise in mothers working longer hours and potentially taking on more demanding roles, with 29 per cent of mothers working full time in 2010 compared to 23 per cent in 1996.

So if dual career couples feel as though they're constantly struggling to do more in less time, that's probably because they are. The work that stay-at-home wives traditionally did – the suppers cooked, school runs organised, PE kit guiltily retrieved from the bottom of the washing basket – hasn't noticeably shrunk, but in some families the time available to do it has effectively halved in a generation. Meanwhile, the pressures of work are squeezing in from both sides. No wonder so many working couples joke that what they really need is a wife: a third person in the marriage, not just to deal with all the dentist's appointments and buying of birthday presents and waiting in for repairmen, but somehow to glue together all the pieces that make up a family. It's less about a desire to retreat to the 1950s than about a hunger for the one thing dual career couples often desperately lack: time.

Fathers may not always be shouldering a fair share of what was once 'wife work', but their time is still stretched increasingly thinly. By 2003, they did around a quarter of the family's child-related tasks during the week and a third of them on weekends, and in couples where both work full-time, men do slightly more than that.[4] The average man still does less than the average woman around the house. But the old domestic bargain between the sexes – you bring home the bacon, I'll turn it into breakfast – is slowly being unpicked, arguably to the benefit of both sexes. And neither employers nor politicians have yet fully understood the consequences.

There are over 12.6 million parents of dependent children in Britain,[5] which is roughly a third of working age adults and a quarter of registered voters: put crudely, that's too many people

for either employers who are hiring or politicians seeking
re-election to ignore. Most of these parents hold down jobs, and
of those who live with a partner, most of those partners will now
have jobs too. No matter how good their childcare, it seems crazy
to assume they can carry on working exactly as sole breadwinners
with the 24/7 support of a wife once did, giving most of their
waking hours to the office. But the debate about working
parenthood is still trapped in a female time warp, obsessed largely
with whether and how women should work, and failing to see
the bigger picture of how men and women in dual career families
now affect each other's choices.

So the big unanswered question from which this book drew
life was not actually about mothers at all. It was essentially the
one that the academic Wendy Sigle-Rushton told me inspired her
own research on marriage: 'I kept thinking, why don't people
ever look at men?' Unpicking the hidden confusion, guilt, distress
and at times anger of fathers – much of which they conceal from
their partners, let alone the outside world – finally helped
everything swim into focus.

It may not feel like it, but the evidence suggests women are
closer than men to securing the family lives they want: men
are now more likely than women to say they want shorter
hours, and less satisfied than women with their current working
arrangements, according to government research.[6] Of course,
some of those mothers probably lose out professionally,
since both the pay gap and the dearth of senior women in
corporate life suggest fathers are closer than mothers to having
the working lives they want. Neither sex has a monopoly on
victimhood. But when mothers miss out on intellectual
satisfaction and financial security at work, while fathers miss
out on intimacy and closeness with their children by spending
so much time in the office, neither sex is really having it all

either. And both sexes are increasingly restless, even angry, about that.

What both men and women now repeatedly say they want is a world where the work of raising children and earning money is shared more equally between both parents. This is no longer some quirky hippy fad, but a mainstream aspiration: eight in ten Britons think that ideally men and women should share responsibility for raising their children and 72 per cent think they should share responsibility for bringing in the family's income.[7] For some couples that is likely to mean splitting things precisely down the middle; for others less so. It's for each couple to decide what suits their respective temperaments, careers and circumstances (not to mention children). But the common thread is a desire to take time back for the family, by sharing the paid and unpaid work in a way that couples themselves feel is fair. And when even the prime minister is prepared to move a Cabinet meeting so that he and his deputy can both do their children's school run, the door is surely open to change in a way it wasn't even a decade ago, when Tony Blair dithered for months before taking paternity leave with baby Leo (and spent most of it working). We are halfway, perhaps, to a solution. But halfway isn't far enough. In this book I want to explore why that change isn't happening faster, and particularly why change at home has lagged behind change at work. For that reason, this book begins with a detailed examination of what has gone wrong for so many working parents, before moving on to ideas for putting it right.

For both sexes, what we say we want isn't always borne out by what we do. Working mothers have been surprisingly slow to see fathers as potential allies in the remaking of working life, quick to scorn their grievances and competitive about who really suffers – even (perhaps especially) with the fathers to whom they

happen to be married. And so the debate about what men do
within family life has become rather angry and critical, focused
on demanding that men do more rather than asking what might
be stopping them. But it took a sexual revolution, sweeping
legislation, the re-engineering of the economy and much individual
female bravery over many decades to reach today's faintly
grudging acceptance of mothers working. Is it fair to blame fathers
when a few largely symbolic and under-funded policy changes
fail to transform them into domestic gods on the cheap and
overnight?

It's true that some fathers, like some mothers, are quite happy
to be absent from their children for most of the working week.
But I think it's impossible to say that's what most men genuinely
want when the disapproval of other men, and the conscious or
unconscious fears of the women they live with, sabotage many
men's attempts to do things differently. While it's still relatively
rare for men openly to challenge conventional working culture,
everything I have heard while researching this book suggests many
are doing so covertly and that younger fathers seem ready to
move more boldly.

So this is not a book about female surrender, about giving up
and retreating to the kitchen: rather, it's about finding a way for
both sexes to embrace the contradictions of work and parenthood,
to straddle two worlds gracefully and still each make time for a
life.

Nor does it seek to stand in judgement on full-time working
parents, or indeed full-time homemakers. Most of us in the real
world don't inhabit such starkly self-confident positions – and
when we do, I suspect we are often subconsciously talking to
ourselves. Nobody is more scathing of the househusband than
the workaholic who fears he secretly missed out on his children,
nobody more vitriolic about the working mother than she who

feels guilty about not contributing more. I have nothing but admiration for couples already perfecting the elusive blend of 100-hour working weeks and blissful family life – but for the rest of us mere mortals, I hope some of the ideas in this book will help. So while the case for more time for parents is sometimes expressed as a warning about the supposed evils of nurseries and nannies, and a presumption that children should be with their mothers at home instead of in formal daycare, that isn't an argument I want to make.

The debate about whether children suffer from their parents' working has raged for most of my life but as far as I can see has barely moved on from Betty Friedan's crisp summary in the 1960s that 'at the present time one can say anything – good or bad – about children of employed mothers and support the statement by some research findings. But there is no definitive evidence that children are less happy, healthy, adjusted because their mothers work.'[8] After years of wrestling with conflicting evidence, first as a reporter and secondly as a parent, all I really know is that I never saw any conclusive proof that working is damaging nor any conclusive proof that it isn't. Like everyone else, I grope my way through this one based on gut feeling, bitter experience, and hope.

But even the psychologist Jay Belsky, who has pioneered work on the damaging effects of daycare, concedes they are fairly minimal. As he put it recently: 'When mothers come to me and say "What should I do with my kid?" I say "The truth is these effects are small enough . . . I don't know if this is a decisive enough finding to tell you what to do with your kid".'[9] This suggests policymakers should worry about the evidence, since even tiny changes in very many children can add up to a significant effect in a population, but that individual parents shouldn't torture themselves over it. When people ask if having

changed the way I work makes me a better mother, the honest
answer is no: sometimes, on rainy days when my son and I are
both bored and tired, I secretly fear I'm a worse one. All I know
is that we are all generally happier and more relaxed without
that sickening, lurching feeling of being out of control both at
work and at home – and like almost all the parents I interviewed
for this book, I can't imagine going back to the way life was
before.

So what I hope *Half a Wife* will do above all is show that there
is life (and work) on the other side. The fable of the high-flyer
who quits is usually told in the media as a taming of the shrew:
female powerbroker sees the light, flees for home and is never
heard from again. A veil is drawn over the most interesting part
of the story, the thing that as a reader I always wanted to know:
what happened next? The answer, surprisingly often, is that the
shrew quietly goes on to succeed at something else, this time on
her own terms.

Contrast the acres of sentimental coverage devoted to mother
of four Ruth Kelly's resignation from Cabinet, with brief mentions
of her subsequent senior position in banking: or take the tale of
Coca-Cola executive Penny Hughes, who worked her way up to
president of the firm's UK and Irish businesses by 33 and then
quit in a blaze of publicity to have a baby. I remember the story
clearly, since it broke during my first year in Fleet Street. What
fewer people know is exactly how it ended. Hughes had her
children, then quietly scooped up several well-paid directorships
on blue-chip boards, achieving a level of corporate success she
has said she would never have managed had she stayed. It is
possible not only to 'lose' a career and regain a life, but for that
life still to include very serious work indeed. The whole point of
a line of desire is that it leads somewhere new, rather than feebly
petering out.

PROLOGUE   11

The weekend I left *The Observer*, I wrote that like many people
I still wanted to work – to do something challenging and
worthwhile – but without it swallowing my life whole. This book,
I hope, tells the story of how to do that.

1

THE LURE OF HOME

It's nine o'clock at night and my son is asleep upstairs, dreaming no doubt of submarines and giant squid. I am in the kitchen, pouring oats, sprinkling sugar, stirring spices into dried fruit and thinking that work comes in many different forms.

I've been awake for about 15 hours, and spent half of them writing feverishly. But there is something in the article that still isn't right, and I am hoping that the pieces of the mental puzzle will fall into place when I'm distracted by cooking, as they often do. After the flapjacks for tomorrow's lunchbox are baked there is just the friend in the middle of the miserable divorce to call, and an email to my sister to send, and possibly a last load of washing to go in. I am tired, content, and some would say deluded.

In less time than it takes just to spread this nutmeg-scented sludge into the baking tin, I could have chucked something ready-made into a supermarket trolley. My son doesn't know or care whether lunch is made by hand (and would almost certainly prefer the sugary packet version, cardboard taste and all). I don't *need* to be doing this, and after a long day I am just creating work for myself. Why?

The sentimental answer would be that I do it for love. But the honest answer is simply that it gives me pleasure: the smell of warm spiced sugar, the magical alchemy of food taking shape beneath my hands, the smug satisfaction of feeling that I am nurturing my son even as he sleeps, and beneath it all the comforting thread of continuity. My mother used to make flapjacks for us, and no doubt my grandmother did it for her. There is the sense of a circle closing, an unbroken connection, a tradition handed on.

But that doesn't quite explain why these things give me pleasure. Why does it matter that it was me and not someone else who coerced my son this morning into painting the splodgy Christmas thank-you letters; me who played games in the bath, read the bedtime stories, fluffed my way through questions about whether there is frost in space and turned out the light? Why do we even want to spend time with our children, given how maddening and draining it can be? And in all honesty, am I happy pottering around the kitchen now partly because tomorrow the virtuous flapjacks will accompany my son to his childminder's, leaving me (as it does three days a week) the equal but opposite pleasure of several hours to work and think and lead the life of an independent adult – a tradition my grandmother most certainly didn't hand on?

The great modern fantasy is of clawing back time for the things and people we love, while somehow not sacrificing status and stimulation at work, and it is a surprisingly unisex one. Business gurus peddle a macho 'four hour week' model of working so smartly that you barely have to work at all – although in reality, those working so few hours a week are more likely to be students pulling pints than successful chief executives. Superwoman has meanwhile been replaced by a less frantic but no less unrealistic role model: the swishy-haired mumpreneurs beloved of glossy women's magazines, apparently running international business empires from their kitchen table while still finding time to supervise their four children's homework. We dream of rearranging work around our lives, instead of vice versa, with almost two-thirds of Britons saying they would ideally like to start their own business.[1]

Nor has this dream of downshifting been as rudely crushed as you might imagine by a recession that should logically encourage employees to cling grimly to any job going. Even at the peak of recession in 2009, nearly a quarter of people still planned to move jobs in the coming year.[2] We are not grateful just to have work, but actually surlier and more resentful. In America, the number of employees willing to go above and beyond the call of duty fell by a third in less than a year as the recession kicked in.[3]

What the waves of redundancies seem unexpectedly to have done is to weaken corporate loyalty, making survivors question what exactly they got back for their commitment to a company now apparently all too ready to drop them in it. Over a third of employees in one American study said the recession had made them feel work was less, not more, important.[4] As one 48-year-old manager who had been laid off told researchers, 'I broke my back for this company, missed my kids growing up, and for what? Nothing!' For years they had made sacrifices for work, only to find that the goodwill they thought they were storing up didn't count for much. It's a feeling oddly familiar to many women who never questioned whether their emotional investment in work was returned – until they became mothers, and were shocked to find that it wasn't.

Some years ago, a female colleague and I had a convivial lunch with a senior woman politician. She was interested in why so few senior political journalists are female, and whether that might change. We chirped up, with all the overconfidence of childless twenty-somethings on the rise, that of course it would – women our age were breaking through and it was surely just a matter of time until some reached the top. Ah, she said, but wait until you have children and see how many of you are left. My friend and I rolled our eyes privately at each other: how terribly old-fashioned.

A decade or so on, my friend and I now have four children and two abandoned full-time jobs between us: that, and the suspicion that she was right. What happened to us all, those parents who disappeared from the professional map? Did we jump? Or were we pushed?

It can be a mistake to romanticise the journey home. For some parents, the 'choice' to quit full-time work is an illusion, the inevitable consequence either of hostile employers or an uglier refusal by their partners to share the domestic burden. They are exhausted swimmers in a rip tide, dragged inexorably away from shore, while their would-be rescuers turn a blind eye – or at worst, hold them under. But the powerful forces pushing us out of work, which will be examined in coming chapters, are only half the story; the rest concerns the lure of home.

We think we understand why some women, and increasingly some men, abandon or change their careers after they have children. It seems so obvious as to barely need explaining: a sacrifice, admirable or regrettable depending on one's view, in the face of our children's need for us and our need for them. Yet in over a year of interviewing parents for this book who had abandoned or changed jobs to spend more time with their children, almost every one has struggled to explain exactly why. Articulate, thoughtful people stumble or become self-deprecating when analysing exactly what it was they felt driven to be at home *for*. Parental love, so ostensibly simple, proves surprisingly slippery to catch under the microscope.

Polly is unusual in being able to identify a moment when things changed, although at the time she couldn't see it. A wry, clear-sighted mother of two girls under seven, her job as a senior executive in a large media organisation meant starting work by 6.30 am. She would often still be at her desk 12 hours later, and taking calls in the evenings and weekends too. Every holiday, she and her husband – a management consultant also working long hours, often away from home – would go round in circles discussing how to carve out more family time. But somehow it never happened, not least because she loved what she did. Even when she found herself working around the clock for weeks, with her parents stepping in to bridge the gap between a full-time nanny and rather more than full-time parents, she was more exhilarated than exhausted.

'The more hours I worked, the more exciting it was, the more convinced I was that I would do anything to make this life work,' she recalls. 'I was addicted.' She took a rare day off only for her birthday, and was planning to savour a lie-in when her elder daughter came into her bedroom just before dawn.

'She said, "Would it be OK if I set the alarm on my clock every morning an hour earlier, so I can see more of you?"' says Polly. 'I thought, she's five years old and she can't even tell the time and her clock doesn't even have an alarm, but she had sat down and worked out how she could see more of Mummy . . . She had thought about how she could fix her life because it wasn't how she wanted it to be. And I just thought: they didn't choose this, and they don't understand it.'

For most parents, there are few things as painful as seeing your child in distress and nothing worse than feeling you caused it, so a hugely powerful part of the decision to come home is our children's seemingly bottomless desire for us. But it's too easy to say that the lure of home is all about the children. The stereotype of tearful faces at the nursery window hides the uncomfortable fact that while some children don't settle in daycare, some happily do – and their differing reactions don't necessarily predict which of the parents ends up with separation anxiety. Even Polly, who seemed to have reached such a clear turning point, readily admits that she actually resigned rather later and only after a long-drawn-out process of talking it over with friends, family and her boss. Some mothers, she notes, welled up when she told them the alarm clock story – but others counselled toughing it out, suggesting the girls were being manipulative.

Lucy is a mother of three, who gave up her academic career after her eldest son was born. Our conversation is regularly interrupted by drilling, as she's managing the renovation of a tumbledown new home in Ireland for the family. Although it's a far cry from their old pressurised life in London, Lucy is still juggling the builders with three children under seven and starting up her own copywriting business. She too tells a heart-rending tale of her inconsolable toddler son crying all day for her at nursery. Yet she wrestled with the decision to stop work for over a year, afraid of doing something she would regret. And there is something apologetic in her voice as she struggles to explain.

'I have my husband's name, but not because it's his,' she says eventually. 'When I came home from the hospital, I had a trauma that I didn't have the same name as the baby. I changed my name even though I hadn't taken his when I married. I just thought, I have to be here with this baby.'

Of course it helps to have a partner earning enough to subsidise such a choice. But contrary to popular belief, it's not just the pampered rich – those who can 'afford to choose', as the bitterly resentful cry goes – who drop out. Far from being trophy wives idling their days away at the gym, full-time mothers cluster around the top *and* the bottom of the household income scale.

Three-quarters of a million lone parents, mostly women and mostly poor, don't work at all: when there is no partner with whom to share the school run or split the summer holidays, all but the most elastic of jobs can be a struggle. Around a million couples with children under five also contain someone who isn't working, and they're more likely to be poor than rich. One recent study found that while only a third of mothers from households in the top income bracket didn't work during their child's first year, four in five mothers in the lowest income bracket didn't.[5] Here is where you find the parents who can't afford *not* to choose home, because they can't earn enough, after childcare, to make work pay. Putting a baby in an English nursery for roughly three days a week eats up more than half the average gross part-time salary,[6] and the tax credits that used to help bridge the gap were cut back last year. Nearly a fifth of mothers in one recent survey said work would no longer be financially viable for them as a result of those cuts.[7]

It's often assumed that poorer women choose not to work because their options are more likely to be menial and badly paid: why not stay home, if the alternative is cleaning someone else's? Yet there is at best mixed evidence that working-class women really put more value on 'the traditional role of homemaking and raising children and having a stable partner so that they could choose how they combine work with what they think of as their great purpose in life, to raise their families', as the former welfare minister Frank Field once put it.[8] My hunch is it's more to do with childcare costs, followed by how you are treated at work, and what your prospects are.

Research conducted by *Working Mother* magazine in 2010 found it wasn't income that determined whether American women described themselves as just working for the money or actively enjoying their career: more than half the happy 'career' mothers (those most likely to be committed to working) were lower earners on less than £30,600 a year rather than high rollers. What mattered was feeling that their work had meaning, and a future.

The balance between work and family is not just tipped by income.

In the end, the closest I can come to explaining what drew me home is a fierce feeling of possessiveness, a rather shameful sense that someone else had something that was mine. Even now, at the end of a working day, there is a small primal shock when my son hurls himself at me smelling faintly of his childminder's perfume. Rationally, I know it's a good thing that she cuddles him; but instinctively, it feels like trespass. He is mine. I am his. At times parenthood is as impulsive and irrational as any other love affair.

And what characterises love – maternal and romantic – is a burning need for intimacy, the time-consuming desire to experience what your loved one does, in the same moment with them: to be inside their heads. 'I love the fact that I'm there from the beginning of the day to the end,' says Lucy. 'I know what all their stories are about. I can see the narrative and the pattern in their days.' As a child grows older, the narrative grows more complicated and secret, but the desire to understand doesn't diminish: parenting teenagers is, after all, partly about knowing when to invade their privacy and when to back off.

This desire to be inside your child's head is partly a protective one, especially as they grow more independent: it's a desperate attempt to see the dangers they might miss, to keep them safe when you are absent. But for me at least it started in the maddening pre-verbal days, when the only way to understand what was wrong with a mysteriously inconsolable baby or incoherently raging toddler was to put yourself in their shoes. When exactly they last ate, how much they slept, exactly which skill they are currently driven mad by being unable to master are all potential clues to the mystery. And to know someone as well as this creates a very particular kind of intimacy. Many mothers talk about waking with a start in the early hours, only to see a baby still asleep at the bedside. Yet within seconds it's wailing. Did you wake because you somehow sensed the baby was going to, or did it wake because it somehow sensed you had woken? It becomes hard to know, in the darkness, where one of you stops and the other begins.

I wouldn't pretend that only full-time, long-term care of a child produces this feeling and it certainly isn't unique to birth parents. But I have other skills like this, so deeply embedded that I don't really know any more how exactly they work – how my fingers automatically find every character on the keyboard when I type, for example – and they're all skills practised over and over again for years until they are instinctive. Going back to work, then, made me feel not so much like a bad mother as like a rusty one. When I tiptoed in from the office at midnight, my sleeping baby would seem distressingly unknowable: mysterious, estranged. Our nanny's meticulous notes of food intake and playground trips couldn't be translated into the nameless things I wanted to know. I felt the ties slackening imperceptibly, became afraid of letting go something I couldn't get back – and of starting to miss my son less, rather than more.

What is it made of, this curious, elusive parental love? There has been an enormous scientific effort in recent years to dissect it, name its chemical components, map its journey through the brain (and perhaps then through society). But just as prising the back off a watch does not reveal the nature of time, exposing the mechanism can't fully explain its hold over us.

The fashion of the last decade has been to explain parental love as all about the hormones, especially oxytocin, the so-called 'bonding hormone' released by women in the presence of their children and loved ones. Even a dog, gazing into its owner's eyes, can increase oxytocin levels in the human brain: it's likely that

dogs have learned over the course of evolution that turning on
the soulful puppy look elicits human affection. Babies certainly
have. Yet oxytocin isn't produced only when we're happy but
sometimes at times of stress, which raises questions about what
it really signifies. Is it a reliable sign that mothers are in love, or
merely frazzled?

Dr Alison Douglas, a neuroendocrinologist at the University
of Edinburgh, and expert on the parental brain, argues that
oxytocin's true role may be in priming the brain to receive other
so-called 'neurotransmitters', chemicals that trigger reactions
within the brain. While it's hard to break down feelings into
precise biological cause and effect, behaviours associated with
parental love – like wanting to be close to a child – are linked to
the presence of both oxytocin and dopamine, a substance closely
involved in human learning.

Dopamine is triggered when we find something enjoyable, from
food to addictive substances like alcohol, and is thought to help
teach us to repeat whatever felt good. The interaction of both
dopamine and oxytocin in activities such as rats licking and
grooming their young suggests caring behaviour may feel
rewarding, encouraging us to do more of it – with obvious benefits
for the survival of our children. These findings have been seized
on in some quarters to suggest women are biologically 'wired' by
their hormones to spend their days caring (and that by extension
men are not). But that's a dangerous leap to make.

After all, oxytocin is also released during orgasm, yet nobody
writes bestsellers claiming women's biological destiny is the blind
pursuit of hot sex. Even Shelley E. Taylor, whose book *The Tending
Instinct* (2002) widely popularised the argument that oxytocin
explains women's tendency towards caring, warns clearly that
'when instinct is combined with the idea of tending, especially in
women, it is a slippery slope to mothering instinct, women's destiny

and other terms that have so often been used to box women into roles they may not choose to play'. Humans are, she points out, still the most flexible species on earth.

Alison Douglas argues that while hormones may be necessary for certain behaviours to happen, experience is also important to 'prime' the brain to receive these chemical messages. 'I see motherhood as a reciprocal combination of biologically and socially determined, including the influence of social or family groups such as sisters, mothers, and other types of social support, including from partners or fathers,' she says. It may be that the act of mothering itself also shapes the adult brain and affects what kind of mother a woman becomes to her next child, she adds: 'A mother's experience of giving care, for example during first pregnancy and lactation [breastfeeding], does cause long-term changes in her brain that then faciliate later behaviour during subsequent reproductive cycles: this is only beginning to be investigated.' Mothers are, in short, not just born but made – by their children, and by the world around them. And that raises some interesting questions about fathers.

Neuroscientists have been relatively slow to explore the 'daddy brain', perhaps partly because typical lab animals like rats and mice aren't terribly paternal. But work on species where males are more active in caring for their offspring, from marmoset monkeys to the California mouse, has started to produce some thought-provoking results. For these animals at least, it seems, being around one's children is part of becoming a good father.

Mouse fathers grow new brain cells in regions of the brain connected with smell and memory shortly after their pups are born, according to research at the University of Calgary,[9] which probably help them recognise their offspring by scent. But crucially, this bonding process only works if the fathers are snuggled up next to the babies in the nest: new brain cells didn't form when they were separated, even by only a mesh screen. Fatherhood also seems to teach mice new skills. Mouse fathers demonstrate better memory while navigating a maze than virgin males,[10] better problem-solving skills (a mouse father, presented with a baby mouse trapped under a cup, will try harder to rescue it than a childless male),[11] and a greater inquisitiveness in exploring new surroundings, which could help mice fathers find food for their families.[12] Researchers in the last of these experiments concluded that fatherhood was linked to 'altered emotionality' in mice.

The bar for good fatherhood is, admittedly, set low in the mouse world, where not eating one's babies is an achievement. There is only so much rodents can tell us about human fathering. But there is compelling evidence that being around a baby alters the human emotional state, too.

Levels of the 'macho' hormone testosterone fall in new fathers, which is likely to reduce a man's aggression, impulsiveness and sex drive – useful for remaining calm around the baby, and faithful to a nursing mother. Lower testosterone has also been linked to empathy, or the ability to understand other people's emotions, which may be important in taking care of babies. Men with lower testosterone levels have been shown to be more responsive to the sound of a baby crying, as have men with high levels of the hormone prolactin, which also rises in new fathers. Scientists are also examining the role of the hormone vasopressin, which in male prairie voles at least seems to be linked with protective behaviour towards offspring.

And like mice, human fathers seem to learn on the job. One experiment involving Magnetic Resonance Imaging (MRI) scans of both new mothers' and new fathers' brains – pinpointing areas of increased blood flow, a crude guide to increased brain activity – found that when they heard a taped recording of their baby crying, brain regions linked to anxiety, arousal and preoccupation lit up in what the researchers call an 'obsessive-compulsive disorder-like manner'.[13] Mothers showed more of this response than fathers just after the birth, but in tests three to four months later, the fathers had developed many of the same brain patterns too. Having a baby seemed to have changed the way their brains actually worked.

Studies commonly involve fathers with young babies, which means we don't know so much about how fathering changes men over the long term. But there is some fascinating evidence linking older fathers' behaviour and hormone levels. One study of Chinese men found lower testosterone levels in fathers than in childless men, as expected.[14] But while in Western men testosterone rises again as the children get older, suggesting the 'domesticating' effect is fairly temporary, there wasn't much difference between Chinese fathers of older children and of preschoolers. Why?

The answer may lie in cultural differences. Chinese fathers traditionally have little to do with babies but spend more time with older children, and the researchers suggested the intimacy of this relationship had increased in recent years thanks to families living in physically small households and to 'changing values regarding the roles of men, and the fact that more women are working outside the home'. Time spent with the children, it seems, might change a man more profoundly than he thinks.

We can't be sure that hands-on fatherhood alters male biology. But findings like these are an intriguing addition to the evidence now piling up for 'neural plasticity', or the idea that the brain is shaped by experience rather than being irrevocably hard-wired with certain personality traits or behaviours. Brain cells can certainly alter the connections they make with other brain cells, and new cells can spontaneously form, throughout life. Although the process isn't fully understood, it appears to be connected to learning new things. It seems the brain may behave almost like a muscle, building extra connections and capacity according to the way it's exercised: what we do, in other words, may determine at least partly what we become. So even quite small changes in men's working and family lives might over time have significant effects on the way they think and behave.

We're a long way from unravelling the biology of paternal instinct, not least because, as Dr Douglas points out, our methods are quite crude: changes in blood flow to a brain region don't necessarily reveal exactly what's going on there. And just as women are more than the sum of their biology, the flexible 'daddy brain' doesn't necessarily steer men into any one fathering role. Better empathetic skills might certainly help a man nurture a baby but they could also arguably help him improve his relationship with his boss, making him a better provider.

But what if it were ultimately possible to show that men as well as women were born with the neurological capacity to nurture, but that in one sex it's encouraged and developed and in the other it isn't? Could there potentially be something as raw and primal about some men's desire to be with their children as there is traditionally supposed to be about women's? The idea is a direct challenge to traditional assumptions about what fathers are for, what they really want – and to the idea that fatherhood is a feeling that can be conveniently switched off between the hours of nine and five.

The classic anthropological view of fatherhood is as a social construct, something men do mostly because society expects them to rather than because they feel biologically driven to it. Pioneering anthropologist Margaret Mead famously put it like this: 'Mothers are a biological necessity. Fathers are a social invention.'[15] Fathers in this scenario are nice to have, but not essential: a back-up carer if the mother is absent or inadequate. Their main role is to provide for the mother, so that she can concentrate on nurturing the children, and it doesn't much matter if 'providing' keeps them away from the children much of the time.

The geneticist Professor Tom Kirkwood has even argued that men may have fewer defences against ageing than women (and so die earlier) because they're less critical to their children's survival: 'Could it be women live longer because they are less disposable than men? This makes perfect biological sense. In humans, as in most animal species, the state of the female body is very important for the success of reproduction . . . a man's reproductive role, on the other hand, is less directly dependent on his continued good health.' One British newspaper reported his views under the stark headline 'Why men are the disposable sex'.[16]

Understanding how experience shapes our brains could start to challenge such views, blurring the line between biology and culture, or between what we 'naturally' are and what the world makes us. If it eventually becomes clear that spending more time with the children produces changes that draw fathers closer to their children, then we might start to question why most fathers are banished back to work after a few weeks, and what would happen if they weren't.

What science cannot, however, yet explain is how much time we need with our children to get the emotional rewards we seek (let alone how much they need with us) and how much we should spend on that other mainstay of human happiness, work. Why do some men and women love their children as intensely as anyone else, but feel comfortable leaving them for 60 hours a week, while others can't bear it?

Guilt is the parent's Achilles heel, no matter how firmly we tell ourselves that there's nothing wrong with working: and one thing that distinguishes the wretchedly guilty from the enviably relaxed is a strong sense of duty. Buried in many of the parents I interviewed was an unusually conscientious streak – a feeling Lee, a single father who withdrew his daughter from nursery to look after her full-time, describes as not wanting 'someone else doing the hard bits' for him – and an anxiety about things spiralling out of control. Professionally, these two qualities make for high achievers who struggle to delegate. Do they make us equally reluctant to delegate care at home?

The great lie successful working mothers tell is that it's all about being organised, when more useful by far is being able to let go and tolerate a little chaos. Deborah Loudon, a mother of two who spent many years in HR before becoming a headhunter, argues that mothers who quit are often the most successful and committed employees, the last people anyone expected to leave. But these are women used to being on top of their game, who can't stand not excelling at both job and motherhood: and the bar for 'excelling' at motherhood is arguably rising.

The time spent by British parents interacting directly with their children has trebled compared to a generation ago despite our changing working patterns, according to one detailed analysis of several thousand time diaries kept by parents.[17] And that reflects a change in how and when we parent. We are more likely now to involve children in what were once adults-only pastimes, like going to restaurants, and we fret about doing endless 'educational' activities with children who a generation ago would have been shooed out into the garden to play by themselves.

Since we're not there all day, as modern parents we bend over backwards to make the precious hours we *do* have with our children count: we haul them round museums, include them in our social lives, agonise over which of the toddler-taming manuals stacked by the bedside to follow. Middle-class parenthood has become more demanding, more intensive, and far more self-conscious, almost a career in its own right. It may seem as if all that stimulation can only be good for our children, but several of the parents I interviewed felt that in the process something had been lost: a certain kind of parenting that involves merely being around, taken comfortably for granted, ignored much of the time but there when a row needs refereeing, they get stuck, or questions bubble up. Small children let slip surprisingly big things on a boring trip to the supermarket.

Susie is a former civil servant, who left her job after giving birth to premature twins, and now works part-time for a think tank. 'That thing of just kicking around the house getting bored, it's something that is at risk of being lost through increasing numbers of parents being dual earners,' she says. 'A friend who has three boys, her firstborn is sitting at the breakfast table every day going "What are we doing today?" and she thinks she's made a rod for her back because she rushed them out to Gymboree and swimming classes and all the rest. I see friends beating themselves up about what they are delivering or not delivering for their children.' While still, of course, beating themselves up over what they are delivering at work.

Olivia is a former HR manager for a well-known consumer brand and the mother of two boys under five. She is a classic example of the woman nobody would expect to fail: efficient and incisive, she spent her first few weeks at home after resigning from a highly pressured job not catching up on sleep, but running through a To Do list of all the things she felt had been neglected. She now works four days a week as a freelance consultant, and our conversation is crammed in on the phone between two client meetings – but the difference is that most days can now stop in time for the school run.

She resigned, she says, because she felt 'guilty at home, guilty at work, guilty on the train there and back. I felt guilty for feeling guilty.' Her watershed was missing the nursery's Christmas party because she got the date wrong, which for her epitomised the feeling of not being the kind of mother she wanted to be: 'I am an organised person and things were falling through the cracks.' Polly, who now works only a few hours a week lecturing, similarly enjoys 'having enough room in my days to do the things I have to do and not being on the back foot. I wasn't very good at being a chaotic mother who does things at 2 a.m.'

But there is more to quitting than being unable to cope with imperfection. The common thread running through all these interviews was a feeling of overload, exhaustion and burnout: families overwhelmed by the sheer number of things to keep track of, the impossibility of being in two places at once, the nagging fear of missing out on something important. And it wasn't just about the children, but something deeper: something to do with home life itself.

What the nineteenth-century American writer Ralph Waldo Emerson called the 'cult of domesticity' – a belief that what is best in life is to be found at home – has an uncanny habit of resurfacing at times of more general upheaval to do with work. It's part nostalgia, part anxiety about change, and partly a sense of dislocation. In Emerson's case it followed the shift from a traditional farming life, in which people remained physically close to home, towards a more distant urban life working in factories. For twenty-first-century parents, this outburst of homesickness seems to have its roots in well over a decade of somewhat turbulent changes to working life, fuelled by the emergence of a globalised economy. We have been swept by a longing, in what suddenly seems like a big cold world, for the small and the cosy and the familiar.

I first became aware of it in my late twenties, back when

marriage and children were a distant and faintly ominous haze. It might have been when the cookery writer Nigella Lawson's baking bible, *How To Be A Domestic Goddess,* came out in 2000 with its siren call for working women 'alienated from the domestic sphere' to retreat occasionally from being an 'office creature' into baking cakes. It might have been when copycat versions of the homewares entrepreneur Cath Kidston's distinctive style – all chintzy peg-bags and polka-dotted teapots – started colonising high streets. It might even have been when my newspaper carried a story about the Egglu, a brightly coloured chicken coop designed for keeping hens in urban backyards, and was deluged with reader enquiries. By the time I was married and pregnant in 2006, the vogue for domestic arts was in full swing and I was raising lettuces in a windowbox. Forgetting Shirley Conran's dictum about life being too short to stuff a mushroom, magazines carried articles about how to grow them.

Why would a supposedly time-starved generation choose such ludicrously time-consuming ways to relax? Supermarket-delivered microwave meals mean we can shop and cook in minutes, yet we have turned food into a leisure pursuit – drifting round weekend farmers' markets like provincial French housewives and brûléeing things for dinner parties. Like the women Betty Friedan observed in *The Feminine Mystique,* still spending as much time on chores as their mothers despite all their labour-saving devices, we have raised standards instead of being liberated from them. The myth is that the new domesticity is all about saving money, but the figures simply don't add up. Dabbling on our south London patio, I soon realised that home-grown strawberries are cripplingly expensive compared to supermarket punnets – and Kidston's quirky fabrics are about buying into a lifestyle, not economising.

The classic feminist analysis is that women are conditioned into this frantic homemaking to distract us from economic competition with men. Is it any coincidence that the cult of domesticity peaked in the 1950s, following a wartime surge of females into work and the need to reclaim their jobs for homecoming men? Or that the home economics movement – arguing that housekeeping was a science that should be taught in universities – emerged at the end of the nineteenth century alongside an awkward female demand to study real sciences alongside men?

We should always beware the velvet trap, the comfortably upholstered prison. But to see the twenty-first-century culture of domesticity as sneaky propaganda for full-time motherhood is to miss the way its profitability depends on working women. This is cupcake capitalism, the reinvention of domesticity as a brisk moneymaking venture: it's all about selling the edited highlights of home life to women too busy for the real thing. My own copy of Lawson's book is now gloopily stained with use, but when I bought it I was childfree and working full tilt. It sat wistfully unopened on my kitchen shelf, a monument to the creative life I didn't have time for – like the kitchen chairs I re-covered in Kidston's striped oilcloth, just before returning from maternity leave. It isn't about the lives we actually lead but about a fantasy of presence in the home, versus the more likely reality of absence at work. The last thing a woman wants for Christmas if she spends her days doing housework is a chintz-clad ironing board.

Besides, men are sucked in by precisely the same cult of domesticity. The rise of the middle-class foodie male, making his own sourdough at weekends, reflects a broader resurgence of interest in the traditional male domestic art of doing things with one's hands. Like the age-old male love of pottering about in the shed with a toolbox, it's about taking pleasure in creativity, in a sense of constancy and renewal. A broken toy fixed, a row of raspberry canes dripping scarlet fruit, is at least something tangible in an uncertain world. And while you don't have to stop work to start an allotment, if your waking hours are almost entirely divided between the office and frantic overcompensation with the children, your fragile tomato seedlings will (like mine) usually die of neglect on the bathroom windowsill.

Such timeless activities connect both sexes, as do our children, to our own childhoods. When the motoring journalist James May launched his television series *Man Lab* in 2010, teaching practical skills like wiring a plug, he was quick to invoke his father's memory: 'My dad is 74 and he worked in industry. He ran steel and aluminium foundries, and with that sort of background he knew how to do stuff. He put the central heating in our house when it didn't have any.'[18] It isn't just what May called 'dad skills' in the home that have been lost, of course, but those jobs in steel foundries too. The decline in manual labour for men has encouraged a romantic craving for working with one's hands that sometimes glosses over the reality of life in a foundry, just as professional domestic goddesses gloss over the realities of spending one's days wiping down worktops. But the championing of dad skills reflects a deep desire for masculine culture to be passed on from father to son, all in the guise of showing him how to put up a shelf. Home for men, just as much as for women, is where memories are handed down and the ties between generations strengthened.

It is impossible to deny the emotional significance of domesticity. Home is inextricably associated in the romantic ideal with love, warmth and comfort. Keep the home fires burning. Home is where the heart is. Home sweet home. Make yourself at home. We make our first homes with those we love, furnish these nests for our babies: we tell our doctors we want to die there, rather than in hospital amidst the professional comfort of strangers. Home is where we preserve our ties to what came before us, and part of its lure now is a pilgrimage back to the home we grew up in. I don't think it is entirely coincidental that I never feel so right about family life as when I do things my mother – who didn't work until I was five – did with me.

Jane, who left a job she loved in the oil industry after having her first child, is a classic illustration of the pressure some daughters feel to emulate their mothers. She feels she did the 'right' thing in stopping work, but finds part-time consultancy in some ways unsatisfying and parts of looking after two small children boring. She wishes she could have her 'brain reprogrammed' to enjoy it more, a clue to how conflicted she feels. It's no surprise to learn her late mother disapproved of working mothers. 'She was a big believer that you should be with babies and small children, with them all the time. She was a trained Great Ormond Street nurse and health visitor, it was a child and toddler development issue for her.' The working daughters of stay-at-home mothers, and indeed the househusband sons of traditional fathers, are like second-generation immigrants, unwilling to turn their backs completely on the culture they grew up in but irrevocably shaped by the different culture in which they find themselves.

Yet at the opposite end of the scale, a home life that fell short of the rosy ideal can also make the lure of home more powerful. Several of the parents I interviewed described a buried desire to rewrite their own family life, this time with a happy ending.

For Neil, a former senior civil servant and father of two small boys, part of the decision to take a job with shorter hours was the determination not to become his own father. 'He saw work as the most important thing in his life and used to tell us that, which was hard,' he recalls. 'He would take himself off in the evenings and go off and do his own work which was largely hobby stuff, it was very much about him – they weren't things that involved kids. There was a distance. When you look back at key moments in your life, like having football trials or exams, I can't really remember my dad being around.'

It was only while writing this book that I realised how both Cath Kidston and Nigella Lawson's careers in domestic blisss were informed by loss: Kidston's mother died when she was 19 and her father slightly after, while Lawson's mother, sister and ultimately her first husband died of cancer. Kidston has said her parents' deaths drove her towards 'things that are cheerful rather than sad. I don't like drabness.'[19] Lawson meanwhile emphasises how making certain recipes evokes the memories of her mother and sister. These women's businesses capture a more muted, undefined sense of loss for a kind of family life subsumed by earning a living.

Yet if the lure of home is really so strong, why don't more of us succumb? Why do the majority of mothers continue to work? Clearly for many there is no financial alternative, if they want to pay the bills. But for the comfortable middle classes, choice is more slippery. Professional women often claim they need to work for the money, but while a salary may be needed to pay the mortgage, did the mortgage really have to be so big in the first place? The hard truth is that many women who say they have to work could have chosen full-time motherhood, but didn't want to make the sacrifices required – no more foreign holidays, or second cars.

And why the hell should they? For generations women put altruistic ideas of care above riches, and much good it did those trapped in marriages they couldn't afford to leave, or financially crippled by a partner's death or desertion. I absolutely do not say it is the wrong choice; merely, that we shouldn't pretend there was no choice. Sometimes it feels easier to claim financial necessity than to admit to the great unmentionable happiness work can bring.

Parenthood *is* work, of course, and hard work at that. But perhaps that's partly why the paid equivalent feels good. There is a reason why mothers describe work as 'me time', complete with the rare pleasure of going to the loo unaccompanied, and fathers volunteer for overnight work trips with their guilty promise of a good night's sleep in a hotel. Sometimes the relative autonomy of work, and the relative simplicity of its demands, may come as a blessed relief compared to the anarchy of home. For while it might look as if parents are in charge, much of parenting is really about losing control rather than gaining it: before you know it, a small person dictates everything from whether you sleep to where you live, and what happens in your spare time. Nothing tests your limits and your patience like having children, and it's this feeling of being out of control that I suspect fuels the surprisingly raw anger often bubbling under the love. It's easier to confess to tearful partings from your children than to the mornings your heart lifted as the door shut, although in all honesty I have had both. But it is as wrong to deny the seductive appeal of work as it is to deny the very strong lure of home.

What stood out in several of the parents I interviewed was a quiet but intense grief for their lost career. They loved their children and wanted desperately to be with them, yet talked about their former jobs as they might have about a lost child; work was the ghost walled up in the attic, the desire for it almost too powerful to admit. 'I miss my job in a horrible, emotional way,' says Polly. 'It feels like I've been dumped by somebody. It's worse than somebody dying: they're around, but they don't want me any more.' She tells herself she is merely taking two years out because she can't bear the thought of never going back, but privately wonders if it will ever be possible: 'The children will still do a myriad of after-school activities; they will have twice as much homework as now . . . I could easily work if I could start at 9.15 and finish at 2.30 but there isn't a job that I want to do that is those hours. I get stuck at that point.'

Some parents of both sexes are perfectly happy to return just as full-time and full-on as before (although as the estimated 30,000 women a year[20] who lose their jobs because of pregnancy could testify, even that's not always enough for their employers). But many millions of parents of both sexes do, like Polly, find themselves continually pulled both ways – lured by home, but also by work and its promise of intellectual satisfaction, financial independence, dignity and self-worth. It's just that they can't find the jobs that allow enough time for both. It's not work we are giving up on, so much as the conventional working day, week and year.

2

CLOCKING OFF

The bank Vicky used to work for has won awards for its family-friendliness, and back in the mid-1990s when she started her family, it was considered enviably ahead of its time. So when she got pregnant, and realised that trying to configure childcare around a commute into London from the Home Counties would be almost impossible, she asked to return part-time from her maternity leave.

Although she had worked hard to reach a senior position in the bank, Vicky was resigned to accepting a sideways move in order to get the hours she wanted. But what she hadn't expected was the bank discreetly blocking every single move she could have made. 'They'd be saying, "Of course, if you find something we will be happy to consider it." But of course, it was difficult to find anything and they never were willing to consider it,' she says. 'I felt it was fine when they were talking about bank clerks or secretaries [working flexibly] but they weren't really interested when they were talking about someone on a management grade.'

Vicky did not go back, and despite working in a variety of careers since has not quite found her niche again. She is left with a profound sense of waste, and of guilt, that she couldn't make it work. 'I have got a decent brain, I could be out there showing that it's possible to have it all, even though I seem to have specifically proved that it actually isn't,' she says. 'I've got a first-class science degree: I could have been using that to do something that might find a cure for cancer.'

Suburban school gates are crowded with people who used to be somebody, and are now mainly somebody's parent. As Jane, the mother of two preschool children, who left a high-powered job in the oil industry for part-time consultancy, put it: 'I find myself in an NCT committee meeting and I look round the table and think "If you collect all the talents that are being put towards running this toddlers' Christmas party, you could be taking over the world."' But while some of these parents are entirely happy with their new lot in life, the sadness and frustration of those who are not is infuriating. The most sobering part of writing this book has been seeing at first hand how much talent, intellect, experience and energy are wasted when parents are pushed out of work they love, often just for want of a little imagination.

It's easy to put the kind of resistance Vicky encountered down to sheer chauvinism, and sometimes that's exactly what it is. Part-time work is heavily associated with women and therefore tainted by age-old female stereotypes: as Vicky found, it's seen as intrinsically less serious, not worth as much. But if a male banker would be regarded with equal suspicion for asking to reduce his hours, then sexism can't be the whole story. And sexism certainly doesn't explain why *men* who work part-time earn even less than women who do so, putting them right at the bottom of the pile: in the UK the average hourly part-time rate is £7.69 for men, £8 for women, and the gap is widening in women's favour.[1] The reduced-hours jobs traditionally available to men appear to be even more low skilled – supermarket shelf-stacking, casual manual labour – than those on offer to women, while the female average is at least dragged up by well-paid professional women wangling a three-day week.

We are not going to get anywhere until we understand exactly why the standard 40–46–40 model – working 40 hours a week, for 46 weeks a year, for the next 40 years of your life – has such a powerful hold on employers' imagination. So in this chapter, I want to examine precisely why full-time working hours are structured as they are for both men and women, and what stands in the way of change.

Human history is littered with grand predictions of a time when mankind would enjoy more leisure, less slog, a magical freedom from the need to make money. The trouble is that they don't quite come to pass. At the height of the 1930s Depression, the economist John Maynard Keynes predicted that by now the working week would be only 15 hours long: we would have learned to meet our material needs more efficiently and would be busy working on 'how to use freedom from pressing economic cares' to do something more rewarding.[2] He was a gifted economist, but a rotten fortune-teller.

Seventies children like me were weaned on the dream that robots would take over the boring bits of working life, freeing humans for endless play, although the only robots we ever saw were the ones on the Smash instant potato adverts. Two decades later came a rash of books predicting the end of the job as we know it: people would no longer be tethered to one employer but would work to what management gurus today call a 'Hollywood model', hired by companies for a few months to take on specific projects and then free to take a few well-deserved months off in between. But although in specific fields like construction and the creative industries something like the 'Hollywood model' now exists, the bigger revolution hasn't quite taken off. Stephen Overell, associate director of the think tank the Work Foundation, points out that the length of time we stay in a given job has barely changed since those Nineties predictions of an end to the 'job for life'. In the year to spring 2011, an extra 35,000 Britons did become self-employed, but still remarkably few of us feel like free agents. 'There's been an awful lot of wishful thinking,' says Overell. 'Big corporates are more powerful than they ever were before and people still want to work for them for perfectly understandable reasons.' One of which being that they can't afford not to do so.

But Keynes was right about one thing: working hours have fallen over the last century. A six-day week was common in Britain until 1912, when the government legislated to allow shop workers a day off in lieu for working Saturdays, and the five-day week we know today only really became widespread after the Great Depression encouraged firms to share out what little work there was. On the surface, we've arguably never had it so good.

Working hours have been steadily falling since the mid-1990s, following the introduction of the EU Working Directive, which limited most of us (in theory, anyway) to 48 hours. One in five of us still do work 45 hours or more, officially considered a long week, but that's down from over one in four of us before the directive came in. And by comparison with our European neighbours, we don't seem to be doing badly: by the end of 2009 only four EU countries – recession-stricken Ireland and the family-friendly cultures of Denmark, Holland and Sweden – had shorter average working weeks than us.[3] We should have felt *less* squeezed for time than we had for decades. But unpicking the figures in more detail shows just how misleading statistics on average working hours can be.

British full-timers do, in fact, still work longer than the European average: we only look good in league tables because we have unusually high numbers of part-timers, working on

average shorter hours than other European part-timers, who skew
the averages downwards. By the summer of 2010, the number
of part-time workers in Britain was at its highest since records
began, with as many people working between two and four days
a week as there were clocking up the classic 45-hour schedule of
the full-time professional. That's partly caused by slumping
demand during the credit crunch driving employers to cut back
shifts, or to smile on requests for three-day weeks that they might
once have flatly refused: a staggering nine in ten jobs created in
the jittery and uncertain recovery of 2010 were part-time, since
it's cheaper and less risky to hire someone for just a few hours a
week if you're not sure how much work there will be to do.

For some parents who seized the chance to negotiate hours
they felt more comfortable with, the recession has undoubtedly
had a silver lining. But it must be said, shortened hours aren't
always shortened by choice: the number of people who wanted
full-time jobs, but could only get a few hours' work a week, has
risen sharply through the recession and many of those affected
are on low hourly wages. Things may change somewhat in a
recovery, but the smart money is on the emergence of a
permanently polarised 'mixed hours' culture, where mini-jobs sit
alongside 'extreme' jobs of 60 hours a week; a nation divided
between minimum wage workers desperate for extra shifts and
happy downshifters, where the time-rich rub shoulders sometimes
uncomfortably with the cash-poor. If this is a revolution in working
hours, it is a very messy and contradictory one.

Whisper it, but employers clearly *need* part-time: one reason
job losses were less catastrophic than feared after the credit crunch
is that employers cut hours instead of posts, avoiding the expense
of laying people off. Yet they don't necessarily need it from those
most keen to give it, with almost one in five requests for flexible
working rejected (although the only reliable research available at

the time of writing predates the recession). Why do reduced hours flourish in dead-end, low-wage jobs and not, as Vicky found, in jobs with good pay and prospects? While the number of full-time working women reaching high-level occupations has tripled in twenty years, the numbers of part-timers getting into these jobs has barely moved,[4] suggesting reduced hours are still not seen as compatible with seniority. We are in danger of creating a two-speed economy, split between part-time jobs – not so senior, not so serious, mostly female – and more prestigious and lucrative full-time jobs most often done by men or the childfree.

Of course parents need to recognise that by offering half a week, they're sometimes leaving their employer to scrabble around for the other half. As Sarah Jackson, chief executive of the charity Working Families, puts it: 'It would be unreasonable to say that as British business works Monday to Friday, if someone works Monday to Wednesday there isn't a gap to fill. It's either by the employee being phoned on their day off or by a job-share or by designing the job so it doesn't need that, and that is a rare job. If you are on the shop floor the company can say "I'm buying 21 hours of your labour": if you're managing the shop floor, it doesn't work like that.' We need to face the fact that not every job can be shrunk to fit parents' desires. Choose to work in certain parts of the City, and you will not be breakfasting with your children: not when the Asian stock markets are open. Becoming a chef similarly means working nights because that's when people eat out, and if you dream of a Michelin star you may want to ponder the chef Helene Darroze's schedule. She has childcare from 9 a.m. to 11 p.m., six days a week, and splits her time between restaurants in London and Paris (she was 40 before she had time to consider a family life, and is now the single mother of two adopted children). But I don't think the scarcity of good flexible jobs can all be so rationally explained away. We need a much better understanding of what really drives us to work the hours we do.

Thinking about this part-time paradox – that employers both desperately do and desperately don't sometimes want less of our labour – I am reminded of a short but vivid phase my son went through as a toddler. All of a sudden, the previously benign sight of me breaking his sandwich or banana up into two manageable halves suddenly filled him with rage. It took me a while to understand that the sight of a half now reminded him that he could have had a whole. So I would end up giving him the entire sandwich, at which point he would usually eat half and chuck the rest imperiously on the floor.

Like the scorned sandwich, part-time comes so often with the ghost of its missing other half attached: a constant, accusatory reminder that you could (should?) be doing more. This is why women say apologetically that they are 'only' part-time: they know it's equated – however unfairly – with half-hearted, semi-detached. This is not a problem for employers filling entry-level jobs, where people tend to come and go anyway: but it clashes fundamentally with the 'always switched on' culture at senior levels. And that's at least partly a problem of perception.

Before I had children I was privately scornful too of the women I knew who vanished into quiet professional cul-de-sacs when they became mothers. I thought they reeked of defeat, slinking off into something second-best instead of toughing it out. But with hindsight, I think they possibly also frightened me: for younger women they served as heads on pikes, a grim reminder that motherhood and career might not be combined as smoothly as we complacently imagined. The supposedly rational business of organising a working day is complicated by some very raw emotions, a point the editor of British *Vogue*, Alexandra Shulman, has made more eloquently than I ever could.

In a forthright newspaper article three years ago headlined 'Why on earth would any employer hire a woman?', Shulman complained that she can forget about getting much done on her magazine during the Nativity play season and argued that a full-time job should mean exactly that, not 'being on the school run at 4 p.m. on Friday when a work emergency breaks out, or making paper snowflakes with your four-year-old while a younger and undoubtedly worse paid and probably childless fellow employee is trying to solve a problem'.[5] Some mothers were, she implied, pricing themselves out of the market with their demands for more time.

It was a little hard not to take this personally. Shulman told an interviewer shortly afterwards that the inspiration for her polemic had been a recent article I wrote for *The Observer* about why I was leaving, so I can't claim neutrality. But Shulman deserves respect as an impressive operator within the British fashion industry, who has remained gracefully at the top of her game in a notoriously tough, results-driven environment despite being, for long periods, a single mother to her son. And what interested me was that the article drew heavily on her own experience of pregnancy in the mid-1990s: her boss was on the phone three months after she gave birth wanting to know when she'd be back, and she duly returned after 18 weeks. Then, she recalled, pregnant women felt obliged to forfeit some of their leave 'out of financial necessity and the sense that that was what one did'.

It is easy to see why some women of Shulman's generation might be irritated by the young women they see having it so much easier now, lolling about at home for a year and then demanding their old job back tailored to fit – after which they might have another baby. There seems to be, rumbling beneath the surface of Shulman's words, an undertone of personal betrayal. 'How cherished does one feel as a boss by someone who is only at work nine months out of three years, the rest being taken as maternity leave?' she asked rhetorically.

Vogue has a 90 per cent female staff, and issues to do with maternity are probably unusually acute. But that's common enough in women's magazines. And there are success stories: Sam Baker, editor of the successful women's glossy *Red*, is renowned in the business for hiring working mothers on flexible terms. *Vogue*'s rival, the fashion magazine *Elle*, was at the time edited by a mother of three who finished at 5 p.m. and had every other Friday off.

Human nature dictates that managers inevitably bring their own gut instincts and assumptions, and their personal histories, to bear on the working day. The male boss whose wife bitterly complains that he's never around may hear a nagging, unintended rebuke in the new father wanting to work from home: the female manager who works all hours can feel implicitly criticised by the new mother asking her for a four-day week. There does seem to be a touchiness surrounding the subject of taking time off for children that is absent when it comes to taking time off for other things, and I think it's because the mention of children arouses strong gut feelings in itself.

High-quality, well-paid, informally flexible work has in fact been quietly available to some people – mainly professional men – for years. It's just that it doesn't involve children. Spending half the day in the pub was acceptable in the Fleet Street of the Eighties and early Nineties, so long as copy got filed: an hour out for something child-related, however, would have been toxic. The rather grand country solicitor with whom I once dealt over a house purchase apparently reserved his Thursdays largely for Rotary Club business, yet wouldn't have dreamed of calling that a four-day week. When non-executive directors join City boards for a few days a month, or Premiership footballers train only in the mornings, it's not called part-time; when deals are sealed on the golf course, or in a lap-dancing club at midnight, it's not called flexible working – as it would be if the deal was done by a woman making calls from her kitchen – it's merely how these things are done. For some reason, working flexibly *around family life* carries a connotation of weakness that working flexibly by itself does not. There is an unspoken inference that rearranging time around your children is feeble, emotional, irrational – and not in keeping with the gung-ho spirit of competition expected from both sexes at senior level.

As the economist Professor Richard Layard, among others, has argued, hours worked are precisely the result of economic competition – basically the fear that if you don't make the effort, rivals will. Longer hours are a way of undercutting colleagues by offering more time for the same money, an appealing deal to employers. A further twist on this is the American economist Sylvia Ann Hewlett's argument that as men are stripped of their unfair advantages over female colleagues – better education, or the chance to get rid of anyone who gets pregnant – endurance is all that's left.[6] Long hours, she suggests, characterise a culture set by the (usually male) senior ranks to weed out competition from (usually female) juniors on the rise.

This economic competition is played out between nations, not just individuals. Last year, when the Indian steel giant Tata cut 1,500 jobs from its British plants, its chairman Ratan Tata complained publicly that 'it's a work ethic issue . . . nobody is willing to go the extra mile, nobody'. It was, he said, impossible to get hold of British managers after 3.30 p.m. on a Friday and staff would leave meetings after 5 p.m. if they had a train to catch. In India, he added, 'if you are in a crisis, if it means working to midnight, you would do it'.[7] Asian workers, he said, were willing to work longer hours than Westerners in general:

'The American will go home and his leisure hours are more important . . . I think there is a certain comfort level that comes from a country that has good times. And there have been countries like ours . . . almost working in a war-like situation.' British parents are used to comparing their working lives, sometimes resentfully, with those of Europeans but it's the culture and choices of parents in Beijing and Bombay – now competing with them in a global market for jobs – that are starting to matter. The recession hasn't just changed the working clock, but redrawn the map, accelerating a shift of economic power from the over-indebted and struggling West towards the still-rising giants of the East.

It's a crude and lazy stereotype, that of the industrious Oriental versus the decadent Westerner. Nevertheless Tata (who is himself, perhaps inevitably, a childless bachelor) raises an uncomfortable question: in the past extreme hours have been associated with national competitive advantage. After all, Britons worked them until well after the Industrial Revolution, when the UK was battling to find its place in the world as India is now.

Working round the clock is also an obvious side effect not just of fast-moving environments where events happen unexpectedly (like journalism) but of the emergence of a truly global workplace. One of London's biggest selling points as a base for international firms now is its time zone, which makes it possible to call both Delhi and New York within a working day (albeit a long one). But working for firms like this means more international travel and more evenings broken by transatlantic conference calls – and it can mean being at the mercy of a corporate culture set on a distant continent.

Dan's old job, working in marketing for an internet company, used to offer a fair bit of leeway for seeing his two daughters before and after work; his original boss was a working father himself, who actively discouraged long hours. But then his boss was replaced by an American with a very different mindset, and Dan was told he would have to spend three months a year at the company's Boston head office. He refused and left to run his own company from home, while picking up the slack of family life with the girls, now aged 10 and 14. What he sees of corporate life through his clients leaves him confident he made the right choice: 'I see the culture – lots of reorganisations, everyone in perpetual fear.'

Long hours are driven by both high and low wages, with the workaholic City trader sharing a similar working day – if he only knew it – to his office cleaner, rising at 4 a.m. to do several jobs since no one minimum wage job pays enough to get by. Long hours also go hand in hand with highly accountable positions, where the buck stops with you, and projects that demand continuity in following the thread from beginning to end. It's no longer solely bosses driving this round-the-clock culture, but clients – which effectively means all of us. Your desire to do the supermarket run at 10 p.m. means some other parent sitting at the till, while clients buying an expensive professional service increasingly expect staff at their beck and call. One former lawyer I know had no trouble securing a two-day week at her firm, but the trouble was, big clients wanted 'their' lawyer permanently on tap and were not prepared to hear it was her day off.

And to be brutally honest, sometimes long hours are nobody's fault but ours: I can easily become so absorbed in writing that I forget to stop and eat. Then there is the perfectionism that made me stay in the office long after others had left, tweaking something nobody else would have noticed. Charitably, this could be called a conscientious streak; or less charitably, a nagging fear of failure.

On the whole I think technology has been a liberating force for working parents, but there is no doubt it increases the pressure to be 'always on', too. Ten years ago, someone might have emailed you at 11 p.m. with a query but they wouldn't have expected a reply until morning. Now, the knowledge that you can pick up the email on your smartphone or home laptop creates the expectation that you will respond. The common part-timer's complaint of cramming five days' work into four (but only getting paid for four) masks the fact that some full-timers are effectively doing six days' work in five – or worse. Lucy, a former academic, recalls being told by a senior colleague when she returned from maternity leave that she should teach four days a week and then do three full days' research. 'And I said "Okay, when do I spend time with my baby?" He had the grace to look embarrassed but that was what was expected, that at the weekends you would be doing your research.' Work is bleeding across leisure time in ways not captured by official statistics, with an increasing confusion over what does and doesn't count as paid work.

For example, in many professional careers there is a twilight zone between work and play which consists of client dinners and drinks, receptions and functions and slightly awkward 'social' events that aren't written into anyone's contract but without which you don't make contacts, get the gossip, or hear about opportunities coming up. (Men who go to the pub at lunchtime with colleagues earn 20 per cent more than those who don't, according to a recent study in the *Journal of Labor Research*.)[8]

This after-work economy doesn't look like work, because it often has all the trappings of fun: food, drinks, chat. But as Tamara Mellon, the Jimmy Choo chief executive who is rarely out of gossip columns, once put it: 'Parties are work.' Or they are if you want to sell expensive shoes to people convinced they're buying into your glamorous life. Unfortunately, this after-work economy clashes with the only time many working parents might see their children. 'The single most difficult thing is I am not swanning around at corporate drinks parties. I could have built a *career* on swanning around at corporate drinks parties,' says Maggie, a part-time public affairs consultant and single mother of one. 'People forget you exist.'

There are many ways, then, in which a parent's desire to shorten or rearrange their working hours after children might fall foul of expectations about what work 'should' look like, especially at senior levels. But it is looking through the wrong end of the telescope to assume that the hours are the only thing driving parents out of conventional work. After all, in centuries past we have put in far longer hours, with a medieval housewife typically rising at 3 a.m. to start her chores. Technically all those brisk time management manuals arguing that if you only laid out everyone's clothes the night before and batch-cooked on Sundays you would have time to learn Mandarin are right – although they miss the point that it's wanting to be in two places at once which is exhausting.

The hidden challenge for working parents is managing the time not over a day, but over a decade. British women now have their children nearly ten years later than they did in the 1950s: the average mother's age at first birth is now almost 30, and for graduates it is on average later, according to the Office of National Statistics. And while reproductive lives unfurl in slow motion, careers have lurched into fast forward.

Women – at least, if they're still working full-time – are rocketing upwards in some FTSE 100 companies now faster than men, propelled by chief executives concerned about boardroom balance: a survey of managers by the Chartered Management Institute in 2007[9] found the average female team leader was, at 37, nearly five years younger than the average male in the same job. Teachers of both sexes now take headships, and businesspeople take non-executive directorships, in their thirties – and while prime ministers were once grey-haired elder statesmen, all three current party leaders are under 45 and have preschool children. Success – and the long hours, responsibility and stress that go with it – is coming earlier.

Major life changes once spread over three decades – from marriage and childbirth in one's twenties to a career peak in one's forties – are now concertinaed for many professionals into one bewilderingly hectic decade, the thirties, when we suddenly try to squash everything in at once. Having enjoyed an unprecedentedly long stretch of footloose living in the post-college years only makes the sudden 'concertina effect' more of a shock. It's hardly surprising if many burn out by 40, prime candidates for dropping out just as it might have started getting easier.

It's timing that makes the choice between parenthood and career so acute, since the nursery years are also those when the stars are supposed to streak ahead of the rest of the pack. Lawyers can expect to make partner on average in their late thirties, the same age as a good senior doctor should be aiming for consultant grade and a City trader calculating whether they have enough money to retire. Even in academia, as Lucy points out, it's no time to take a career break: 'Every four years you have to account for your research: where it was published, how much you have done, and that's entirely a quantitative system. There is room on the form to say "she was off on maternity leave for a bit" but anybody who drops work really, really struggles to get taken seriously. I know academics who have decided not to have children because of the research exercise.' I was once asked in a radio interview whether my boss had been brave to make me political editor at the age of 33 – by which the interviewer clearly meant an age when I might have children. Then, I was too shocked to answer properly. Now I would say we hear too much about the risks employers run in hiring women of childbearing age and not

enough about the risks employees run in cramming everything
– excelling at a job, hunting for a mate, buying a home, children
– into one tiny window.

The concertina effect isn't all bad news for women, of course.
In previous generations many were lost to motherhood before
even getting near senior positions, whereas now they're within
sight of promotion when they get pregnant. But for men, it's a
profound shock. The critical phase for career lift-off comes just
as spouses are pushing them to leave work in time for the nursery
run: what many men hear is a new and angry demand to be at
home more, coupled with an older and contradictory demand to
earn more and support the new family.

The concertina effect also squashes together the age of
childbearing with the classic age of professional disillusionment.
With midlife milestones looming, it's natural to take stock and
reconsider job choices probably made rather hastily over a decade
ago, which is why the thirties (along with the fifties) are a peak
time for career changes even among the childless, according to
headhunters. It's when many people start wondering if they can
really stand another three decades of this job before retirement.
A striking number of the parents I interviewed admitted that had
they not had children, they might naturally have been looking to
move at the age they actually quit.

In her study of why women leave high-pressure 'extreme jobs',[10]
Sylvia Ann Hewlett found that the desire for more time with their
children came top overall. But for women in business specifically,
'career not satisfying' came top instead. A quarter felt 'stalled in
their career', almost as many as those who cited the pressures of
looking after elderly parents. In other words, some are leaving
for exactly the same reasons as men have always left jobs, but
they also have the nagging parental tickertape running in their
heads – the daily question, *is it really worth leaving my child for this?*

Many of the parents I interviewed described having no tolerance for the petty irritations of office life – pointless meetings, cumbersome bureaucracy, time-consuming office politics – once they were racing to leave the office in time for nursery pickup. 'I don't think anyone can prepare you for the exhaustion, and the sitting in a meeting where somebody's snivelling on about something trivial and you think "I will be late home for *this*?"' says Olivia, who left her job as an HR manager to work freelance. 'My tolerance for anything that wasted time went right down. I'd think "I'm not having meetings about meetings."'

And for some parents, work is now quite literally less rewarding than it used to be. Even at the height of the boom years, low and middle earners were already quietly going backwards in pay terms: salaries for the 'squeezed middle', as these now understandably angry voters are dubbed, stopped keeping pace with inflation three years before the credit crunch began. Now these same parents face a triple whammy of nursery bills rising above inflation, cutbacks in the tax credits that used to subsidise their places, and what might be several years of pay freezes. Some are bound to conclude that work simply no longer pays. In August 2011 an analysis from the think tank the Institute for Public Policy Research warned that working mothers were already dropping out of the job market as a result.[11] But the twist is that this problem is no longer confined to mothers.

The dilemmas faced by fathers who want to spend more time at home are subtly different from those faced by mothers, and they are not nearly so well understood. But they belong right at the heart of this unfolding story.

3

DADDY WARS

Fatherhood, when it came to Lee, came almost wholly by accident. He was only 26, working and playing long hours in the pub trade: none of his friends had settled down yet, and he hadn't been with his girlfriend for long when she got pregnant. He didn't necessarily want a baby. 'I had never connected with babies, and sleepless nights and the teething and the constant storm of shit didn't appeal,' he recalls. 'I wasn't expecting to be a dad.' Nonetheless, he knuckled down to the idea, assuming that life would carry on much as normal for him: his partner would stay home with the baby and he would continue in his job running a pub restaurant.

The first shock was his daughter's premature birth. The second was two social workers arriving with an emergency protection order. Unbeknown to him, Lee's girlfriend had a child from a previous relationship whom she was accused of harming and she was deemed a potential threat to their daughter. Suddenly, he found himself the primary carer of a three-month-old baby.

'She did the nursery thing for a while and I went to work but I hated it, although looking back I am not a natural parent with babies,' Lee says. 'It just didn't feel right. Initially my way of getting through the day was to think "I have to work so I have to

put her in nursery, and it's horrible but you just have to do it."
But someone else was raising my baby. Whenever I dropped her
at the nursery she was happy and gurgling but when I went to
pick her up – in all honesty it was probably the time of day, but
she was never that excited to see me.' Although the brewery let
him work 9-to-5 at first, Lee quickly realised he couldn't run the
pub properly without being there on weekends and busy nights.

Unable to reconcile his feelings for his daughter with the three
hours a day they managed to have together, Lee took what he
thought would be a year off to be a stay-at-home father. Six years
on, this rugby-loving, self-described 'blokey bloke' is a full-time
single father to a little girl who is, as he puts it, 'all about the
fairies and pretty sparkliness'.

It hasn't been easy. There were legal battles over establishing
custody, and life remains a far cry from what he was raised to
expect; Lee's own father suggested he have the baby adopted. It
has been an incredibly tough learning curve and even now, Lee
worries he isn't good enough at the glittering and sticking and
fiddly craft activities she loves, despite the home-made fairy badges
drying in the kitchen as we talk.

But it's clear they have a close, loving relationship. 'I wouldn't
change it for the world. As much as life now is not perfect, she
knows that I am here for her and she knows I have got the
experience of watching her grow from that puking little baby into
really quite a lovely little girl.' As for Lee, he has grown too: 'My
reality changed. Who I was, was no longer who I was.'

But sadly the man he is now, while infinitely more versatile,
no longer seems so employable. After struggling to find pub
catering work that didn't mean long antisocial hours, he diligently
retrained as an accountant when his daughter turned three. Three
years later, he still can't find work and is living on benefits.

Lee is oddly more encouraged when potential employers

question outright how he'll cope with childcare as a single father: at least it means that, for once, they're not automatically ruling him out. Despite a carefully worked out childcare plan involving after-school clubs and emergency backup, he is gloomily realistic about how employers see him. 'As a former employer, I know you discriminate against single parents because you can't question it if a single parent phones up and says "I am not coming in, my daughter's sick",' he says bluntly. 'I have lowered my bar so many times it's ridiculous. My plan was to be an accountant; now I'm applying for anything and everything.' Yet after hundreds of applications he has so far been offered one job in Canada – which he couldn't take – and an unpaid internship he can't afford to do.

It is impossible to hear Lee talk about his daughter without realising that men are every bit as capable as women of the loving, nurturing care that is so often thought to come 'naturally' only to mothers. But it's also impossible to hear his story without understanding why more fathers don't choose to give that care. He estimates that single fatherhood has 'cost' him up to six figures compared to what he would have earned by sticking to the conventional path. His story helps explain why something about modern fatherhood just doesn't add up.

On the one hand, young men almost certainly give more time now to their children than their fathers and grandfathers did: by 1997, British men spent eight times as long with babies and young children as they had done twenty years before.[1] That's still less time than women, but it's no longer novel to find men on the school run, in the playground, or even chewing the fat on Mumsnet (a little over 5 per cent of users are in fact dads).

Attitudes are arguably changing even faster than behaviour: more than half of men across Europe now say they approve of fathers looking after children and home,[2] something almost taboo in their grandfathers' day, although perhaps only about 3 per cent of British men actually do it full time. And fatherhood has become a much more physically intimate process. More than half of fathers, in an extensive study of 10,000 new parents funded by the Department of Health,[3] were there when the telltale blue line appeared on the pregnancy test and almost nine in ten attended at least one ultrasound scan, a ritual perhaps more important to men than we think. The reason so many men cry when they first see that grainy blur on the screen is that it's often the first time the unborn baby becomes as tangibly real to them as it is to the woman carrying it.

Once the baby was born, more than seven in ten mothers in this study reported, their partners helped 'a great deal' when the baby cried, while more than half bathed the baby equally often: these fathers weren't just grudgingly changing the odd nappy, but genuinely trying to get to grips with their newborn. More than half of the fathers went on to look after the baby 'a great deal' while the mother was out or at work, and for those taking paternity leave, the average was four weeks – two weeks over the statutory minimum, suggesting they used holiday time too.

It's hard to say how exactly this has changed from equivalent fathers a decade or more ago, because although this thorough study of all aspects of women's experience of having a baby has been repeated three times since 1995, nobody thought to ask about the fathers until 2010. But the psychologist Charlie Lewis's groundbreaking 1986 study *Becoming a Father*, which looks at the generation by whom today's new fathers were largely raised, found that over half never looked after the baby on their own and fewer than a third bathed the baby a lot. No wonder many men resent being criticised for not doing their share: if they compare themselves to their own fathers, rather than to their partners, they probably feel positively revolutionary.

My guess is that official statistics on men reducing their hours are not necessarily telling the whole story. The work patterns of low-paid men in particular may mean they can spend a fair amount of time with children without having to ask for it; they're more likely than professional men to work shifts, and so to be around in daytime more, or to be among the 'underemployed' unwillingly working part-time. And if their partners also work alternating shifts, there is often no choice but to share childcare. Men like this might not be able to afford to take paternity leave, but still probably see more of their children than the father who ostentatiously takes a fortnight off before resuming 14-hour days.

When I interviewed Charlie Lewis shortly before beginning this book, he suggested that while professional dads talk a good game about hands-on fatherhood it's working-class men who more often quietly practise it: 'The lower you go down the earning spectrum, the more likely you are to find people doing childcare.' He cites a pioneering survey of unemployed Newcastle men in the 1990s, who did the bulk of childcare and chores while their wives worked. Yet they resisted the label of househusband, insisting they were just helping out a little.

Some professional fathers too are redrawing their working lives by stealth, in ways that aren't always recorded in statistics. They will ask for (or quietly take) flexitime informally, rather than lodging a legal request; or duck promotions that would take them away from home more, without necessarily explaining why. (Half of American fathers with one child now say they wouldn't take a new job offering a worse work–life balance, according to research by the management consultants McKinsey.)[4] Sometimes, they simply vote with their feet. 'If you ask men, they will often say the reason they left was to look for a more flexible workplace,' says Rob Williams, chief executive of the Fatherhood Institute charity, which lobbies on behalf of fathers. 'They may not feel able to challenge the culture where they are, but they will leave.' I've certainly known a fair few new fathers suddenly and inexplicably decide to leave newsrooms for the more fixed hours of PR.

But there is something strangely private, and silent, about the way men tackle this dilemma. When I wrote for my former newspaper about my own decision to leave full-time work, I was astonished by the torrent of letters, emails and texts I got from fathers confessing to all the same doubts and fears: many said it wasn't something they would discuss with male friends (and still less with their wives), leaving them sadly isolated. The fierce camaraderie between working mothers does not seem to exist in quite the same way between new fathers, and there is little sense of an organised movement for change, although some individual men are increasingly prepared to acknowledge publicly what their careers have cost them.

Sir Howard Stringer, the chief executive of Sony, shuttles constantly between continents for work and has described spending only a few days a month with his wife and two children. As he once told a meeting of company workers, 'I don't see my family very much: my family is you.' Questioned about those rather stark remarks, Stringer has said he uttered them with sadness: 'This is a tale repeated around the world with all of these globetrotting business executives. You don't quite know what I'm inflicting on my children. And so I overcompensate when I'm around them, and I tend to walk in with bundles of Sony devices as a sort of social bribery.'[5] Men have more insight into the impact of their hours than women think – but they can't afford too much insight if they want to run companies like Sony.

This explains the rather puzzling gap between what fathers say they want from work, and what they actually *do*. According to government statistics, in 2007 14 per cent of men had tried to change their hours in the previous year (against 22 per cent of women),[6] but the men were more likely to try and vary their hours if they *didn't* have children than if they did. Fewer than half of fathers regularly even manage to read a bedtime story, perhaps because many still aren't home until the children are asleep. Are men kidding themselves about how much has really changed?

Rob Williams was recently invited to hold a seminar on family-friendly working for men at the big City bank, Merrill Lynch, and was heartened to find the room packed. 'The managing director of Europe and the Middle East stood up and did a big speech on how they were really keen on flexibility. I asked people to put their hands up if they were fathers and they all did,' he recounts. 'I asked them to put their hands up if they had arranged to change their working hours and one hand went up. It was the woman from HR who had organised (the seminar).' As Williams adds: 'Although they think they've entered this new world, if you pin them down they haven't really.'

Charlie Lewis was similarly pessimistic about the 'new dad', pointing out that even in the 1970s, 5 per cent of fathers did more childcare than their partners; three decades later, it's still only about 15 per cent. Brave talk by modern liberal dads often conceals more conservative practice, he admitted. 'I think it's great to have equality in the home. But I work all the hours I can get and I leave my partner to do everything I can at home.'

What would men really do, if they didn't need to work for the money? Nearly half of men in a 2009 British poll would go part-time if money was no object,[7] while a quarter wouldn't work at all. Fathers were keener than men in general, and *just as keen as mothers*, to give up work completely if they could afford it, although the headlines following this survey were all about women's yearning for home.

But fathers of the youngest children, those under 11, were more torn. They were even keener than mothers to stop work altogether if they could, perhaps because surveys show that men typically enjoy their jobs less than women. But these newer fathers were also keener than men in general to work full-time if money were no object, suggesting that for some the office might be a positive haven compared to the noisy chaos at home – or else that the idea of fathers needing to be 'providers' is so deeply ingrained that it persists even when they don't need the money. How to make sense of such a hopelessly contradictory picture?

Untangling it requires accepting that not all fathers are the same. Just as some new mothers sink blissfully into domesticity while others smuggle laptops into the maternity ward, there is a wide spectrum of fatherhood, stretching from the devoted stay-at-home dad to the absentee workaholic (or the divorced father who abandons his children). Some fathers are happy working all hours, while some would doubtless be happy never to work outside the home again, which makes it is as meaningless to generalise about 'what men want' as it is to generalise about women.

But I want to focus on the muddled majority in the middle, the men being pulled in two directions at once. The argument that these fathers freely choose to work all hours because that's how they like it echoes something often said about women choosing to be at home: that they're 'naturally' made that way. As we saw in the first chapter, it pays to examine the idea that anything is 'natural'. The assumption that men are instinctively more detached from their children conveniently ignores the way they are moulded by their upbringing, culture, partners, financial circumstances and in particular by competitive pressures from other men.

One reason that mothers so often change their lives dramatically after having children is that pregnancy is a big enough shock to reset the clock. Mothers are hatching reinvention and drama from the minute a pregnancy test bisects their lives into 'before' and 'after': it's almost impossible to feel the piercing heartburn, cramped lungs and trampled bladder of late pregnancy without wondering how this unborn child currently rearranging your internal organs will end up rearranging your life. And after birth come months of limbo in which to ponder blearily how much you do (or don't) miss work, alongside an overarching social expectation that life will not be the same again. What struck me about the fathers I interviewed who had made big changes was that they had also often experienced a shock jolting them out of the unthinking pattern – redundancy, personal trauma, changes at work, or simply a financial squeeze which trumped other considerations. It made me wonder how many men might question the assumptions of a lifetime were they given cause to do so. Can we really say that the traditional way of fathering is a free choice? Or is it, like a woman's 'choice' to quit a hostile workplace, a murkier thing altogether?

In her 2003 study on the modern 'intimate father', sociologist Esther Dermott concluded that men who love their children but feel obliged to be separated from them by work may try to rationalise things by arguing that time together isn't really important. The fathers she interviewed wanted to be involved with their children, but defined that as having a good emotional relationship rather than necessarily seeing them often: 'Rather than fathers having an idea of intimacy which is impossible for them to achieve in reality, they may be satisfied that their behaviour does adequately express their deep attachment to their children.'[8] It's a convenient way of resolving their feelings about not being around as much as they might like, since they have seen what happens to those colleagues – nearly always female – who do seek to spend more time at home.

'Men understand that one of their advantages over their female colleagues is that they have got the freedom to work,' says Rob Williams. 'When they ask for flexibility, they understand that they are crossing an unconscious line and declaring themselves not to be always relied on to be there at nine o'clock at night.' And crossing that line means inviting themselves to be treated as badly as they've sometimes seen female colleagues treated. Yet we wonder why so few men use the supposedly unisex right to request flexible working.

One reason men make fewer formal flexible working requests than women is that a large volume of requests are from existing part-timers, mostly female, just wanting to tweak their hours. But full-time men who ask are still *twice* as likely as full-time women to be turned down.[9] Men are more likely than women to work for inflexible employers, who don't offer many ways of working, and more likely to be senior, when flexibility is easier for juniors to get; but there is almost certainly some inbuilt resistance too to men who go against the macho grain. The biggest reason men give for not asking is 'business reasons', otherwise known as the fear that management won't wear it. Why endure the mutual recriminations and loss of face that go with asking, if the answer will only be no?

Jason is a sheet metal worker by trade, married to a teacher, and the couple have two daughters under five. When his wife returned to work after maternity leave with her second child and the girls went to nursery, pressure on the family ratcheted up to virtually unsustainable levels. 'Everything was a rush all the time. We would get up in the morning and it was a rush to get them dressed and to have breakfast, and a rush to get them out of the door, and a rush to pick them up and a rush to get their tea.' Their two little girls were, he says, 'bouncing off the walls' with tension. So Jason asked for flexitime at the factory where he worked, to fit round the morning nursery run.

He was only the second man in a factory of several hundred workers to try and change his hours, and the only one on the factory floor: he simply wanted a slightly later start and finish time, rather than reduced hours, but still his foreman balked. 'He said: "I'm not having that, I am not having you being a part-time worker",' Jason recalls.

Undaunted, Jason appealed higher up and won, but it wasn't forgotten. 'Whenever there was a problem or something went wrong he would say, "What are you on about, you part-timer?" and I would say, "I do exactly the same hours as everybody else."' Jason ended up racing to reach work only 15 minutes late and staying a full 30 minutes longer at the end, effectively doing unpaid overtime – a scenario many working mothers will recognise.

What clinched his decision to leave was when Jason realised the £1,300 a month he made after tax was swallowed up by mounting childcare and petrol costs. Effectively, the family gained nothing by him working. And since his wife Cathy, a teacher, is the bigger earner, the couple decided Jason should become a full-time father.

He was surprised to find how little he missed work, and describes movingly the experience of watching his two little girls grow up and forge their relationship as sisters. 'I'm very happy with the decision we made. There is the odd day where I do think to myself "ooh you little buggers" but I thoroughly enjoy it: it's time we will never have again.' But although he wants to find a job fitting round school hours when the girls are older, Cathy worries he'll never earn again what he did at the factory. 'We have made this decision knowing we are pretty much going to be scratching around for money now for ever, although we don't regret that,' she says. It's female-dominated professions like hers which are usually best geared up to cope with maternity returners, and although male-dominated industries such as banking have begun to woo returners back, schemes are usually aimed at lost mothers rather than fathers.

Women reading this may be tempted to think: welcome to my world, buster. For decades, having children has jeopardised women's careers, and it's usually been men who benefited from them dropping by the wayside. It can be hard to feel sorry when the tables are turned. Why can't they brave employers' hostility just as women have always had to do?

But women need to rise above their scepticism, and not just because men have as much right to a full and happy family life as they do. This is a golden opportunity for working mothers to make common cause with men who increasingly share their interest in the way time at work is used. After all, causes are liable to be taken more seriously when twice as many employees espouse them, and – unfairly – sometimes also when men instead of women complain. Profoundly irritating as it can be when the man taking an afternoon off for sports day is feted for his domestic godliness, while the woman doing so gets nothing but snide comments about another missed meeting, it can only be to both sexes' ultimate benefit if family life is 'normalised' at work. (If nothing else, every father parading his halo on sports day means one more mother who didn't have to rejig her diary for it.)

But to forge alliances like this, both sexes have to stop competing for 'victim' status and recognise that each faces pressures that the other doesn't. A successful woman who compromises her career for the children will often be praised for doing it, because she is conforming to a sentimental idea of what 'good' women do. A man doing the same, however, is challenging the idea of what it means to be a man: competitive, ambitious, and a successful provider.

Dan's wife has long been the big earner in their relationship, and at first he describes his previous job in marketing as one he didn't particularly enjoy but 'did for the money'. Then he corrects himself: given his wife's salary, they didn't need the money either. 'You know what? It was partly because there is something in our culture that says "I have to have a job". I didn't have to work, but as a man I felt I had to. Really I could have been in Caffè Nero with the mums.' The association between having a child and providing for it is strong enough to defy financial logic. And turning your back on it isn't easy.

Neil is a father of two boys under four, who was until last year working as a senior civil servant in a stimulating job with frequent travel, long hours and high stress. Despite a nagging feeling that the job was putting family life under strain, it was only when he was made redundant that he had time to reconsider. The traditional choice would have been to carry on working similar hours for rather more money in the private sector; instead, he deliberately went to work for a charity, which offered fixed hours and one day a week working from home – plus the chance to do something he believes in.

There have been, he says, 'golden moments' with both boys since. 'You can just allow yourself to relax into their world more. On a Saturday morning I can just sink into making some enormous Lego thing with them for an hour and a half, not checking the BlackBerry or obsessing about what might be happening.' What is noticeable about highly involved fathers is they describe time with their children almost exactly as women do: precious time too easily lost in the rush.

Still, even though he and his wife are happy with their family life, Neil is conscious that his new job lacks the cachet of the old. 'I often wonder what other people think: "he isn't ambitious enough or he's somehow not capitalised enough on what he did or he's failed to take a big step forward"? I think they're wrong, but I do worry about it, no question. There's a macho thing about it, although I sort of think I have been quite brave.'

The word 'macho' is revealing: men who work unconventionally often fear the slur that what they do is unmanly, emasculating. Women gush enviously over househusbands, but the respect of other men is still closely linked to money and status. When Jason resigned, the factory's female director of personnel told him warmly what a great thing he was doing. The male managing director, he recalls, 'just said "You're doing *what?*"' His male colleagues, too, couldn't really understand why he wanted to be at home: 'Somebody said to me "You picked a great time, the World Cup's on."' Dan similarly says that while dads on the school run are perfectly welcome in his corner of liberal north London, he is teased by old friends about his wife being the major breadwinner while he works part-time from home: 'Some of my friends take the piss. I have quite a few friends in the City and that's a bit unreconstructed: I get quite a lot of jokes from them about being a househusband.'

Sadly, men are right to fear that active commitment to their children may make them vulnerable, and nearly always to other men – mostly those who work long hours themselves. I was halfway through writing this chapter when I heard BBC Radio 4's *Today* programme discussing attempts by Nick Clegg, the deputy prime minister and a father of three, to control his working hours. The interviewee was David Mellor, perhaps best remembered now as the Cabinet minister who resigned over a fling with an actress. Mellor's stinging comment that 'we live in PC [politically correct] times when having a young family can be used as an excuse for not working hard' would have caused uproar had it been said about a working mother; aimed at a father, it was barely challenged by his interviewer, who is a father himself.

Even the liberal *Guardian* newspaper has been drawn into the sexual slanging match, with a male columnist dubbing the Labour leader Ed Miliband a 'wuss' for taking paternity leave: when the government announced last year that a father would have the right to six months' parental leave with a new baby if his partner went back to work, one anonymous reader of the *Spectator* magazine's website accused ministers of giving 'girly-men other people's money to stay at home when their spouses pup'. Men in real life experience some of the same sideswiping.

The vitriol is fuelled, I think, partly by an age-old antagonism towards wives who decline to surrender their own career and support their husbands. When Clegg's lawyer wife Miriam Gonzalez described last summer how he still 'killed himself' to do the school run, her husband was described by a female *Daily Telegraph* columnist as a 'supine weakling' but it was Gonzalez who was accused of being 'militantly ball-breaking' and blamed for making him do it. His 'sins' remarkably quickly became hers. But I think there is more than covert misogyny going on here.

What Americans call the 'mommy wars', a clash between working and stay-at-home mothers over whose way of life is morally superior, is arguably overhyped; although the odd bout of one-upmanship is an inevitable fact of playground politics, most of the mothers I know are too busy worrying about their own family lives to waste much time bitching about other people's. But there are definite battle lines being drawn between 'traditional' fathers, who may have worked long hours when their children were small, and those now seeking to spend more time at home. And the extraordinary vehemence of these emerging 'daddy wars' suggests a strange kind of suppressed panic.

It's oddly reminiscent of the zeal with which some cultures police women's dress and morals, which is often really all about men's fear of losing control, of their rational behaviour being swept away by desire. I suspect what's fuelling the daddy wars is fear, too: fear of change, fear of difference, fear of being 'unmanned' by independent women, and a niggling fear among men who have worked long hours themselves of what that might have done to their children. And mixed in is, I think, a deeper fear of parental love itself: a fear that it could drown men as well as women in its intensity, if they let it. As the writer Anthony Giardina puts it in his essay 'A Brief History of the (Over)involved Father', explaining why he prioritised his career when his second child was born, 'I have used my identification with Homo Fifties . . . as a kind of guardianship against excess, a handhold to keep me from slipping entirely into the much-desired embrace.'[10] After all, if fathers are indeed more inherently detached than mothers, why does our culture expend such an enormous amount of effort on keeping them at arm's length?

The idea that mothers are 'necessary' to children but fathers more dispensable is ingrained in most men from childhood, not least by their own fathers. Lee's father, a solicitor, was always 'working or at the golf course. I saw him on weekends for a couple of hours.' Even that was progress, since a generation before Lee's father had had to book an appointment through his own father's secretary to convey the news that he had passed his law finals. 'My grandad just said "Derby winners breed Derby winners, son",' Lee recounts.

Boys learn what it is to be a man from their mothers, too. For all my own liberal theories, I can't help noticing that my son's toy box seems to be overflowing with robots and trucks, not dollies. It's tempting just to marvel at the unstoppable biological tide of *boy*, since these are the toys he craves, but I realise now I made rather sketchy efforts to encourage more 'nurturing' toys from the start. And while mothers have grown wise to the dangers of filling little girls' heads with tales of passive fairy princesses, we've been less alert to the surprising lack of domesticated literary role models for little boys. Mothers in children's books tend to be as saintly and comforting as stepmothers are wicked; fathers, however, are often loving but comically useless.

Think of the Gruffalo, snoring idly in his cave while his offspring strays alone into the deep dark wood; or the fat buffoon Daddy Pig in the popular preschoolers' cartoon *Peppa Pig*, or even the elephant father in Jill Murphy's charming *Mr Large in Charge*, left to supervise his brood while their mother is ill. He burns their lunch, injures himself on a garden rake, lets them break the vacuum cleaner . . . no wonder the children keep rushing plaintively upstairs to her. As for the father in 'Hansel and Gretel' who abandons his trusting children in the woods in order to please their jealous stepmother, I found rereading that as a parent downright creepy.

It sounds petty, but stereotypes – whether of domestically incompetent men or helpless but beautiful princesses – can be surprisingly powerful. Women do significantly worse on science tests when they're previously shown images of ditzy women.[11] They score best if gender isn't even mentioned, suggesting even the subtlest prompt can shatter confidence. Black students score higher on a miniature golf test when told it's assessing sporting ability (fitting the stereotype of black men as 'natural' athletes) than when told it's a puzzle-solving exercise.[12] It's hard to believe that the domestically clueless stereotype has no impact on men, and their willingness to get involved at home, or that it doesn't encourage them to compete on the more certain terrain of work, where the odds still seem stacked in their favour. There are precious few examples for men of how to be 'good' at family life, and precious few chances to practise in advance.

Contrary to popular male opinion, women weren't born knowing what to do when a baby has a temperature: these things were painstakingly *learned*, and not just from reading the baby

books (the intelligent ones marketed at mothers, not the insufferably
dumbed down ones for dads) or listening anxiously at antenatal
classes. Most women first learn to change a nappy or reason with
a toddler as teenage girls, earning pocket money by babysitting,
yet many otherwise liberal parents instinctively feel uncomfortable
about hiring teenage boys to do the same. And while young
women are always welcome to cluck over a strange pram in the
street, our national hysteria about paedophiles means young men
lack opportunities to get close to children, or even imagine how
life might be with them: just watch the way mothers in an urban
playground react if an unaccompanied male lingers by the fence.
A heartbreaking little report from Play England, the charity
promoting safe play for children, published during the hot summer
of 2010 found almost half of men questioned would now avoid
a child apparently in trouble on the street lest they be accused
of taking an unhealthy interest.

Looking back through my own newspaper cuttings, I'm struck
by how often I used the phrase 'working mother' in an article
about new legislation or research when I should really have said
'working parent'. It was never intended that way, but I see now
how it unconsciously pushes fathers away. And that does make a
practical difference. Rob Williams of the Fatherhood Institute
points to one experiment where instead of addressing appointment
letters to 'Dear Parent', health visitors began addressing them to
'Dear Mum and Dad' and saying they looked forward to seeing
both parents at the visit. Significantly more men turned up when
the word 'dad' appeared in the letter. It's not enough to be gender-
neutral about family life: fathers need to be explicitly invited in,
not least because it is increasingly obvious how much children
gain as a result.

Children who spend a lot of time with their fathers tend to
have better verbal skills, probably because men use 'baby talk'

less than women. Children whose fathers are the main carer show greater belief in their ability to control events, which may be linked to fathers' higher expectations: watch a toddler in the playground being egged on by its father to stunts its mother would forbid, and you see how fathers might foster confidence. Older children who say they talk to their fathers about things that matter to them have higher self-esteem and better general well-being than those who don't.[13] And since one study found a father's interest in his child's education, particularly around age 11, had a stronger influence on educational success than family background, poverty or the child's personality, one could even argue that a distant father working all hours to pay the school fees might do just as well coming home early and supervising homework.[14]

Slowly but surely, this idea that fathers' time – and not just their money – is valuable is moving out of academia into the mainstream. Images of hands-on dads sell anything from cars – with a recent American advert for Ford featuring a father teaching his little boy to ride a bike – to life insurance: Zurich Help Point's campaign at the end of 2010 featured a huge, rather moving black and white photograph of a father nose-to-nose with a small baby. (David Cameron was photographed in a similar pose with his newborn daughter, Florence.) And fathers' time is now considered enough of a social good for governments to promote it.

In Japan, where the intense corporate culture of long hours is thought to fuel a dwindling fertility rate, the government recently funded a website promoting the image of *ikumen* – a word which means roughly 'househusband' – and encouraging men to take parental leave. And in America, the state-funded 'Take Time to be a Dad' campaign screened in 2010 showed fathers playing and bonding with their children in various all-American ways – fixing a torn teddy bear, cheerleading, playing drums in the basement. The campaign was endorsed by President Obama, whose close relationship with his two young daughters is a key part of his electoral appeal.

Obama's own father left the family when the future president was two, and Obama Junior has campaigned eloquently for fathers to support their children. On this side of the Atlantic, it always struck me as interesting that two fatherless boys grew up to be two of the Blair government's fiercest advocates of fatherhood. John Hutton's father walked out on his five children when the young John was 12 and never paid maintenance: nearly four decades later, as a Cabinet minister his son legislated to put fathers' names on birth certificates and pursue non-payers of child support. Hutton's colleague Alan Milburn, also raised by a single mother, ultimately resigned from Cabinet saying he was missing out on his two sons' childhood. My generation of fathers was the first to experience, as children, the mass absence of fathers through divorce: and I suspect that for some the result is a subconscious urge to build fathers back into the picture. During the moral panic over parenting that followed several days of rioting and looting in British cities last August, it was noticeable that accusing fingers were for once, whether fairly or not, pointed at absent fathers as well as single mothers.

In short, men now experience many of the same cultural pressures as women to be more involved parents – but an equal and opposite pressure not to do so, for fear of jeopardising their role as providers, which women are less likely to feel. No wonder many men embark on fatherhood keen but baffled, hopelessly unsure of their footing.

For the first few weeks, new parents now mostly stumble through it all together: both flip frantically through the baby book at 2 a.m. trying to work out what's wrong with the purple-faced ball of fury, and neither really knows how to collapse the pushchair. Yet once the few short weeks of paternity leave are over, the world divides like a segmented orange. Men return to the hard-edged world of work, and so many women float off in a pink bubble of new 'mummy friends', their own mothers, female health visitors and mornings spent in buggy-gridlocked cafés. Living this strangely female life after so many years in the grittier climates of journalism and politics was a shock for me: it deepened my relationships with my mother, sister and friends who had children in profoundly moving ways, but I had never felt the world so rigidly divided by gender – or so separated from my husband's. How does it feel for fathers, trapped on the other side of the glass?

So much conventional baby wisdom seems to make Daddy the enemy, too. The classic advice for getting older babies to sleep through is for the breastfeeding mother not to respond to their cries, sending the father in with a bottle of water instead. It works, but the lesson for the baby is that Mummy is the reward and Daddy the punishment, offering nothing worth having. As the child grows older, discipline is often slyly ceded to the father at the grumpy end of a toddler's (or teenager's) day: he becomes the enforcer, she the comforter.

And consciously or not, the 'mummy network' of playgroups and coffee mornings can still exclude fathers just as sharply as the old boys' network excludes women in the office. Lee quickly became disillusioned with the playgroup scene: 'Women don't half moan, and mostly about men. The sole purpose of toddlers' groups is for women to moan about their partners.' He tried a single dads' group but found he had nothing much in common with them either: at-home dads are still rare enough for the chances of finding a kindred spirit to be small. One househusband I know, meanwhile, recalls mothers physically leaving the sandpit when he and his toddler joined in, 'like I was about to *pounce* on them'.

But it's time that does most to strengthen the maternal bond at the expense of the paternal. After up to a year of Mother at home and Father at work, she's the one who can open the buggy with the flick of one hand, who knows which lurid vegetable mush is preferred; he's the one rummaging around during nappy changes, not sure where the wipes live. And unsurprisingly, she has often become the firm favourite.

Polly, the former media executive, says one reason she quit her much-loved job rather than her husband leaving his is that it wasn't him the children wanted. 'He took two months off during the summer between jobs, and even with him at home all day the children cried for me and didn't want me to go out,' she says. 'The thing they needed was Mummy. I can't explain that. I am not a better mother than he is a father, I'm not kinder or more patient nor do I have less of a temper.' She may well, however, have a history of early intimacy that was hard for her husband to match. My own son wails for Mummy in the middle of the night, not Daddy: but when my husband spent a few months at home while this book was being written, I was surprised by how quickly my son began seeking out his father for some things; surprised and, if I'm honest, sometimes faintly hurt.

There is a small, martyred part of many women that loves to be needed: it can be horribly gratifying to be the expert at home, especially after a long day of being made to feel unwelcome at work. Maternal gatekeeping, or the art of subtly refusing to surrender the baby to anyone else, is a serious obstacle to involved fathers. As one of the wives in Charlie Lewis's study, *Becoming a Father*, put it: 'I didn't want anyone else to feed [the baby] but me, but I used to think he ought to.' And what women too rarely acknowledge, when they sacrifice their jobs to spend more time with the children, is that in doing so they may be making their partner's choices for him: if she isn't going to earn, then the pressure rises on him to earn more, regardless of how much that may take him away from his children. Too often women have choices, and men merely responsibilities.

Yet the life of a househusband married to a female breadwinner can be hugely rewarding, as Jason found; and this arrangement can be all that makes some extreme jobs feasible for women. As businesswoman Cynthia Carroll, a mother of four and the highest ranking woman executive in a FTSE 100 company, put it in a recent interview: 'I'm a very engaged mother but my husband has worked from home ever since I have been running global businesses. Women need that set-up or it doesn't work.' Nonetheless, men at home full-time are running the same risks that full-time housewives always have, from poverty in old age to boredom and isolation – plus the threat of being unable to support themselves if their partner dies or divorces them. They also have the strain on both sides of bucking convention. It can be difficult for men to let go of other people's expectations that they 'should' be earning – but difficult for women to let go of the children too.

Jason thinks Cathy would love to be a full-time mother if she didn't earn more than him. There is, he admits, 'a bit of conflict' at weekends when she does things differently than he would during the week. He says she can be irritable at the beginning of the week, missing the girls after spending the last couple of days with them. And Cathy says while she's extremely grateful for Jason's sacrifices and thinks the arrangement suits their strengths – she was, she thinks, 'vaguely depressed' being at home with babies – she can't escape a nagging feeling that she should be home instead. 'Rightly or wrongly, I don't think he missed them in the same way that I do and they don't cling to his leg in the same way they do to me,' she says. Although Jason's career change has relieved pressure on the family, it hasn't really taken a different pressure off her: 'My entire focus is the kids: I do all the putting them to bed and bathing because I want to. By the time I've come down from that and particularly if I have to do some work, I haven't got any time left over. I do feel a bit drained and I do feel that I am not giving him enough time.'

The mixed messages that women often unwittingly send about what they want men to do are critical to understanding the contradictions in modern fatherhood. For it's not just their children that men seek to please by investing time at home, but their wives as well.

The anthropologists Peter B. Gray and Kermyt G. Anderson define fatherhood essentially as a mixture of parenting effort (the basic desire for one's genes to survive) and 'mating effort', or a cunning strategy to get sex.[15] If women are motivated by protecting their children's welfare, then nurturing those children might logically encourage her to stick around. Good fatherhood is quite the effective seduction technique, which is perhaps why so many new fathers find walking down the street with a baby strapped to their chests generates a startling amount of interest from young women. But a few months on, they may find that doing what they thought was required of a 'good father' – working hard, chasing promotion – suddenly generates a startling amount of fury from their wives. Confusingly, what men were brought up to offer no longer seems to be what women want, or certainly not all they want, although this economic effort still wins the respect of employers and of other men. And that leaves men torn not just between work and their children, but between the approval of men and the love of women: and increasingly, between work and their marriage.

4

FOR BETTER, FOR WORSE

There is a dirty little secret shared by too many overstretched working couples, far harder to confess than the commonly acknowledged guilt about the children. And it's the guilt about what has happened to the love affair between the parents.

Last year, the relationship guidance charity Relate identified long hours as one of the five most common problems affecting clients, up there with infidelity and redundancy. Yet while it's socially acceptable to say you are cutting back on work for the sake of the children, adding 'and the marriage' takes things into murkier territory. It's not just embarrassment about confessing to a rocky patch that keeps couples from talking about this, but the fear that changing a job to benefit a relationship sounds so feeble: it smacks of a surrendered wife (or downtrodden husband) pandering to a selfish spouse. What fool would invest in love, over the economic certainty of a career?

The complex ways in which paid or unpaid work impacts on relationships, and relationships in turn affect the time and energy we have to work, are the untold story of modern family life. Denise Hall, a Relate spokeswoman who has been counselling couples for nearly twenty years, says couples might not always identify long working hours as a problem at first but it often emerges at the first session: 'It will be "you spend more time at work than you do with me", "you don't do enough round the house", "you're never there", "we don't have enough couple time" – and 99 per cent of the time, the reason for that is work.'

The couples she sees are struggling both with women's changing roles and, she thinks, with a new urgency about work. 'Less job security and more job changes: a feeling that you need to get to the top pretty fast, that you need to secure it now because if you don't get this company off the ground someone else is going to do it.' She has also noticed couples travelling more intensively for work, and being away for longer.

For all our focus on maternal guilt, a survey of 4,600 American working parents found women felt worse about their relationships with their spouses than about their childcare arrangements,[1] an indication that it's often the marriage that sinks to the bottom of an overflowing To Do list. Some men, too, are becoming willing to acknowledge what work has done to their relationships. Sir Stuart Rose, the chairman of Marks & Spencer, confessed in an unusually candid interview that his first marriage failed because 'I let it go off the rails . . . it got to a junction, and I could have done my happy-go-lucky Stuart bit, or I could have done my achiever bit. I was wrong.' His subsequent relationship with the fashion writer Kate Reardon failed, he added, because 'at the time M&S was my wife and my mistress too and Kate got what was left, which was very unfair'.[2]

Yet few of us talk really honestly about the impact of work on relationships. It's a delicate subject because the blame for relationship breakdown is still too glibly – and often unfairly – pinned on women working, with a lingering inference that it's their fault for 'neglecting' their man in pursuit of a career. As the TV presenter Lizzie Cundy told *OK!* magazine, after her

Premiership footballer husband's decision to end their marriage, 'Jason said I took my eye off the ball.' It's obviously quite wrong for women's work to be tolerated only if it doesn't interfere with getting dinner on the table. But I think there is a bigger question lurking here.

A little over a decade ago, the celebrity divorce lawyer Vanessa Lloyd Platt wrote a rather explosive article for the *Daily Mail* arguing that the husbands of working women were increasingly seeking divorce because they were tired of always coming second to a career. I was working for the paper at the time, and remember floods of letters from female readers, many of them divorced: the angriest were usually stay-at-home mothers, who had put their family first only for their husband to leave. Yet some divorcees wrote, in self-lacerating detail, to agree. Had they merely swallowed their husbands' self-justifying versions of events? Or if we leave gender out of it and consider the effect of both men's and women's single-minded pursuit of demanding careers, is it possible to acknowledge that between them they can push some marriages to breaking point?

One study of workaholics carried out at the University of North Carolina found their spouses had fewer positive feelings towards their partners, significantly lower attachment and less desire for emotional intimacy than the spouses of people not addicted to work. Marital estrangement – a gulf between husband and wife – was common in the workaholic marriages and they were more than three times as likely to divorce. The workaholics' partners were also more likely to feel their lives were not under their control, presumably because work often disrupted everyone's plans.

Clara is a former solicitor, now a full-time mother to three children and a foster mother to many more, who says that at times her husband's all-absorbing job running a large organisation tested their relationship. 'The phone never stopped – these people didn't respect weekends, evenings, it would be a Sunday morning at 9 a.m. and the phone would start and just ring all bloody day. Every time we wanted to do anything with the family he would be there with the phone under his ear. It was like they owned three-quarters of him, and I had the other quarter if I was lucky.' It isn't just overstretched executives' marriages that are at risk, either. Among low earners, taking on two jobs just to make ends meet 'was a cause of resentment, and meant people were often tired and their relationships suffered', according to focus groups conducted by the think tank Resolution Foundation at the height of the recession.[4]

Work can save a marriage rather than kill it, of course. Dual earners are often better off than single earner families, and they do at least avoid the frustration of a spouse who wants to find a job but can't. Besides, some time apart is probably healthy for most relationships. But how much time apart is too much?

According to the writer Camilla Cavendish, a former management consultant with McKinsey, the firm once calculated that marriages were potentially endangered when workers clocked up 65–70 hours a week.[5] For the workaholic, spending so much time away from home may mean more opportunities to meet someone else: for the spouse, all those dinners burned, cinema tickets cancelled, holidays wrecked and hours wasted waiting for a partner to peel themselves away from the office cause festering resentment. But depending on how many hours that spouse is also clocking up, the crunch may begin well below 65 hours a week. One reason, I think, that many of us instinctively feel working life is getting harder despite the recorded fall in working hours is that the statistics only capture hours racked up by individuals, not by households. Working 45 hours a week may feel perfectly manageable with someone at home picking up the domestic slack – but it may feel very different if that person starts working 45 hours a week too.

Wars break out when there is intense competition for something in short supply, from fertile land to oil, and for working couples that scarce resource is time. So many marital battles are about what both partners do with the limited and pressured time available outside work – especially if one spends it doing chores, and the other maddeningly avoiding them.

Nicola returned to her job as a social worker when her daughter was only three months old, because she didn't qualify for full maternity pay. At first she worked three days a week and coped well enough, but the cracks soon set in at home.

'When I was back at work I thought that would mean we'd be sharing the childcare 50/50. That didn't happen, because I was still breastfeeding, I was up most nights . . . I was really, really tired and not getting a break. He was still going out with his friends. Resentment just built up and up, and by the time she was about 18 months we had gone from being a couple that shared everything to me being a housewife with a job too,' she recalls. 'The nursery would ring me, not Mike; even the cleaner would leave notes for me, not him. It had become a huge respect issue: "If you loved me, you'd help . . ." We never came back from it, really.' The couple had split up by the time their daughter was two.

Very few of the partnered mothers I interviewed voluntarily raised the domestic burden when discussing why they left work. Yet when asked, time and time again they would loyally say their partner was hands-on, before promptly suggesting the opposite.

Lucy and her husband, both academics, see their relationship as based on egalitarian principles. She says he is 'really good' around the house, then goes on to list what he doesn't do: 'On a Saturday the clothes are washed and sorted but they won't be put away, they won't make it on to hangers. He has broken the Hoover every time he touches it – he doesn't hoover.' Initially they had agreed he would look after their baby son a day a week, but 'I would say he was there five weeks out of 25. They always have the flexibility of passing it on to you and not feeling funny about it – not having that sense of "but I should be there, I should be doing it". He'd say "I've got work to catch up on this weekend so are you going to your mum's with the kids?" but the other way round wouldn't happen.' Yet they both had similar research responsibilities and at the time she earned more than him. As she puts it, 'Being married to a Marxist feminist is kind of handy, but the Wigan man surfaces from time to time.'

Liz, meanwhile, was working full-time as a voluntary sector executive when we spoke, and her husband is a lawyer. She describes him as 'very hands on' with the children when he's there: he cooks sometimes, and cleans up after dinner. But he won't pack his own suitcase for a family holiday, and before her last work trip she had to prepare all the PE bags in advance because he doesn't know what goes in them. Last Christmas, Liz bought all the family presents and had them delivered to the office, setting aside one night to stay late at work, wrap and label everything. 'I expected Michael to come and at least put labels on so he knows what he's bought for his mother for Christmas. He couldn't fit it in because he was too busy with all the drinks parties,' she says drily.

It seems Liz taught herself, eventually, not to mind. 'I am much more pragmatic about it now than when we first got married. I won't have a row for the sake of it. I would be permanently arguing, or nothing would get done, or I would get more stressed.' Interestingly, some months after we spoke, Liz told me she was quitting her job and looking for something more flexible.

Olivia, a former human resources manager and mother of two

children under five, has similarly conceded defeat. Although at times in their marriage she worked longer hours and earned more than her husband, who ran a succession of business start-ups, she describes having long taken on most of the domestic responsibilities: 'My husband is quite relaxed about a traditional set-up [at home] but also very relaxed about me earning shedloads of cash. I have given up on the tiredness competition.'

Had her marriage improved since she resigned her corporate job, and set up as a part-time HR consultant? 'My husband would say things have vastly improved. I would say I made a decision at the same time as giving up work that it was ridiculous me fighting over him doing 10 per cent. I have just accepted that that is who I have married. I have adjusted my expectations of what he is going to do from 10 per cent to zero and life is much easier. There is a clarity to it. In a way it's fair. I am much less guilty and I think guilt is a horrible emotion. It makes you horrible and scratchy.' As, of course, can anger.

From the outside, it's easy to wonder why women don't put up more of a fight. But the stubbornness, the anger, the sheer dogged passive-aggressive resistance of some men to doing their fair share at home can be formidable and exhausting. Sometimes it's easier just to stack the dishwasher yourself than fight for half an hour about whose turn it is. After all, a husband who fails to pull his weight when asked is essentially offering his wife three grim choices: to cope with everything herself on top of work, shrink work to fit around everything else, or leave. It may sound crazy, but many women would rather cut their hours and work around the husband than confront the possible end of the marriage and the consequent risk to their children's security.

One EU-wide survey asking what would most help improve work–life balance showed that people were less likely to cite a fairer distribution of domestic chores in countries with lots of part-time jobs, such as the UK and Holland.[6] There was far more concern about who does what at home in countries where mothers have longer working hours, such as Spain; in Romania, the issue was deemed as critical as tackling the pay gap. The widespread availability of part-time work, which clearly offers more time to fit in the chores, seems to defuse domestic anger. But is that a healthy thing, or is going part-time really for some women a way of ducking awkward questions about who does what at home?

The hardest question I have had to ask myself while writing this book is how far that was true of me. There is an argument my husband and I have been having now for at least a decade and it runs in wearily familiar circles around the fact that I have done more, and he has done less, around the house for as long as we have lived together. I have shouted, pleaded, nagged; I have cried, wheedled and sulked. I have bribed and threatened, gone on strike, drawn up endless indignant lists consisting of long sprawling columns (my domestic contribution) versus a few brief sentences (his). And mostly, I have failed. Or I had until this book began to take shape, and it became obvious that conflict over housework is too dangerous to ignore.

When the academic Wendy Sigle-Rushton began studying the relationship between housework and divorce, her original aim was not relationship guidance but to challenge a Nobel-Prize-winning economic theory put forward by the economist Gary S. Becker. According to Becker, marriage is like the relationship of two trading countries: it works best when each specialises in what they're good at and barters the rest. The breadwinner earns and the homemaker nurtures, trading pay cheques for freshly ironed shirts or child-rearing for having the mortgage paid. Becker argues that this should produce efficiency gains for both, since the breadwinner can maximise income for the whole family now he's free from domestic cares. This delicate balance of trade could be wrecked however if one partner muscled in on the other's specialism – if, say, a wife gets a job. The rising divorce rate, Becker's theory suggests, could reflect modern women's refusal to specialise.

One problem with Becker's elegant theory is that if lovers behave like countries, they're often like rich Western nations trading with exploited Third World states: the breadwinner's 'efficiency gains' aren't always equally shared with the homemaker. Bringing home all the money may make him feel entitled to decide how it's spent – and as some divorcees have found to their cost, what is his won't necessarily be hers for ever. But the lightbulb moment for Sigle-Rushton, a senior lecturer in gender studies at the London School of Economics, was realising that if Becker was right, divorce rates should also logically rise in couples where men do more housework: after all, they've stopped specialising too.

When she analysed the responses of 3,500 married couples with children aged five and over to Household Survey questions in the 1970s, Sigle-Rushton found that marriages did indeed founder more often when women worked.[7] But they actually became more stable than average when the men helped out at home. His willingness to do chores seemed to offset the risk created by her working. In couples where he did very little domestically and she worked, the risk of divorce was almost double that of the most stable relationships. It's not just a woman's changing role that endangers the marriage, but a man's inability to change in response to new circumstances.

The Household Survey doesn't record why these marriages ended. But as Sigle-Rushton told me, 'Having the man involved tends to make women happy – and women tend to be the ones who instigate divorce proceedings.' Sharing housework may well be one of the most powerful ways to insulate a marriage against all the heartache, expense and social cost of divorce. Yet unlike infidelity or marrying young, the impact of the so-called 'second shift' done by women on top of work is a marital risk factor most couples go to the altar knowing little about. Even couples who start off willing to pull together at home can find themselves divided and conquered in unexpected ways.

It's not just work that sometimes separates parents from each other and from their children, but the physical geography of our lives which, in the words of six leading architects, 'creates enormous rifts in people's emotional lives. Children grow up in areas where there are no men except on weekends; women are trapped in an atmosphere where they are expected to be pretty unintelligent housekeepers; men are forced to accept a schism in which they spend the great part of their waking lives at work and away from their families and then the other part of their lives with their families away from work.'

The archaic language gives the game away: it's from the 1977 book, *A Pattern Language*, which describes a new way of thinking about architecture designed around how people actually want to live. These days women aren't all marooned in suburbia, nor men all estranged from their children, of course, but the physical distance between work and home still affects the time we have for each other and the roles played within a marriage.

The average commute for a British worker is now 27 minutes each way, and over twice that for Londoners. One in 20 have a round trip of over two hours a day,[8] and in the pretty west Oxfordshire villages near me, a round trip of four or more hours isn't unusual. Rising property prices in the established commuter belt have pushed families further and further out, with counties as far-flung as Suffolk and Somerset now seeing influxes of London season ticket holders.

Among the hardest hit by extreme commuting are the low paid: junior public sector workers who need the extra allowances paid for working in the capital, but can't afford to live there any more. Half of Metropolitan Police officers now commute into London and it emerged during an industrial dispute among London firefighters in 2010 that almost half of them don't live in the capital either, commuting in for blocks of shifts from as far afield as Blackpool or Scotland. (London firefighters earn over £5,000 a year more than those from other brigades, and the average terraced house in Blackpool costs over £200,000 less than one in London.) Extreme commuting makes economic sense – but it carries an emotional price.

In 2011 a Swedish researcher concluded that those commuting for more than 45 minutes each way were almost half as likely again to get divorced in the early years of a marriage as non-commuters. One reason, she suggested, was that commuting could 'sustain gender-based stereotypes both at home and in the labour market'.[9] If a man commutes (and it is more often men who do) then the need for someone to be around for school pickup may push his wife into working locally, where her pay and prospects are more limited; he, meanwhile, may get home at 9 p.m. tired, resentful and reluctant to help at home in what's left of his free time. He becomes trapped in the role of breadwinner, she in the role of primary homemaker (although often with a job as well), and it's the simmering resentment as well as the lack of time together that hurts. The cruel twist is that such extreme commuting is often prompted in the first place by having children: fleeing big cities for better schools and idyllic rural childhoods often means a gruelling trek to the only job that pays the surprisingly expensive rural mortgage.

Once upon a time, merely having children made marriages less likely to fail: couples marrying in the 1960s were statistically less likely to divorce if they were parents.[10] By the 1970s, this protective effect was still evident when children were under four, although not for those with older children. But for couples marrying in the 1980s, parenthood suddenly became risky in itself: those with two children, at least one a preschooler, were 17 per cent *more* likely to get divorced than childless couples.

The 1980s mothers were perhaps more likely to work and to be able to support themselves: arguably, they had greater economic freedom than 1970s mothers to leave. But that really only explains why parents should become as likely to separate as childless couples, not why they became more likely to do so. Work is only half the story; and I think the other half involves what happens at home.

Sentimental expectations that parenthood will bring happiness are not borne out by the evidence. Happiness tends to dip during the child-wrangling years, the thirties and forties, and peak in the teenage years. Parenthood is associated with being slightly less happy than being childfree, especially for those with toddlers and teenagers – the two stages at which children most test our patience, and most need our time.

The free time available to new parents shrinks alarmingly as the work at home mushrooms: the once-weekly laundry that's suddenly twice daily, interspersed with what a friend once called the 'endless wiping' – snotty noses, bespattered highchairs, sticky handprints on the wall. But what children do above all is turn time within marriage into a zero-sum game.

Before children, an adult's freedom to follow hobbies, see friends, devote time to work or to themselves may have to be negotiated with a partner but doesn't have to be traded so remorselessly. But as soon as one of you needs to babysit for the other to go out, one person's freedom is bought at the expense of the other's. Becker was right about one thing: home is where parents trade, not just in time and money but endlessly and more subtly in worth. Every argument about who can do the school run tomorrow, or who was supposed to get more milk is a trade in which we attach value to each other's time and other contributions. To claim his Sunday afternoon football takes precedence over her right to a long, hot childfree bath, or that her meeting can't be moved so he should cancel his is to infer something about whose time is worth more, whose status is higher and who has most 'earned' (by paid or unpaid work) a break. The endless ensuing competition – who's more tired, more overworked, more deserving – is corrosive.

A study of full-time workers carried out by the University of Pittsburgh School of Medicine found that household chores made blood pressure rise faster than work meetings. The worst affected were those who felt they were shouldering the most responsibility, not necessarily those spending most time on housework.[11] It's the feeling of injustice that rankles, whether for the woman lumbered with the loo brush or the man nagged into cleaning when deep down he feels that working all day long should be enough.

Men are not as oblivious to this domestic battleground as many women think: asked to describe possible advantages of flexible working, four out of ten men say having more time to share family tasks, suggesting they do see chores as a source of tension.[12] But they may still not really understand why. Rob Williams, of the Fatherhood Institute, says most men genuinely don't see the connection between what they do around the house and the state of their relationships; all they know is that they keep getting shouted at. 'Men feel nagged. They feel that their partner's changed hugely whereas they haven't changed at all, so it must be their partner that's the problem not them,' he says. 'They can't understand the causational chain they are involved in because it's never expressed in a way that might allow them to link up the fact that they are not doing any childcare with the fact that their partner is angry with them.' The trouble is that to men and women, domestic work often means completely different things.

For women, caring for a home and children involves more than practical necessity. Cooking a meal means nurturing those around the table, not just feeding them, and even tidying up signifies the creation of a relaxing environment for others. Housework carries an emotional significance for many women, who are culturally conditioned to see caretaking as an expression of love, so when their partner doesn't do any in return they feel insulted and rejected. But for men, chores are just chores, and low status ones at that – one reason why many would rather hire an (almost invariably female) cleaner if their spouse feels overburdened than do it themselves.

Culturally conditioned to see providing as an expression of love, men tend to offer paid work as their 'gift' to their partner – even if she also works, even if she earns more. It's why men put photographs of their children on their desks to motivate themselves and why the England cricketer Andrew Strauss plays with his wedding ring tied on a shoelace round his neck, 'to remind me of why I play cricket – for my family, my wife Ruth and my boys'.[13] I suspect it's also why some men feel aggrieved about being expected to do housework on top of paid work, even (quite illogically) if their wives do both. Denise Hall of Relate says the complaints she hears about long hours come not just from neglected or overburdened partners, but from aggrieved men who feel that they 'shouldn't be expected to do 50 per cent at home' if they're already working hard. They've shown love by providing: why, they wonder, have they got to do it all over again?

So women offer care, and feel hurt and angry when all they get back is wet towels scattered on the floor. Men offer hard work, and are bemused and angry when all they get is a lecture about not being home on time. Trading like this is not the smoothly ordered market envisaged by Becker but a black market swap conducted by two people guessing wildly at the exchange rate, both suspicious they're being conned. These tensions may have existed before parenthood, but they are thrown into sharp relief by the arrival of children and perhaps by the shrinking of our social horizons that often comes with it. Home takes on an awful lot more significance when you are suddenly spending much of your time there, instead of being part of a bigger and more sociable world.

Parenthood, according to one study for Co-Operatives UK, costs one friends: it found the average childless couple has 4.7 close friends, compared to 3.5 for a couple with three children.[14] And that's not counting the many more casual relationships that fall by the wayside. During the manic years, my friendships certainly became measured in snatched mobile phone conversations from the back of a cab, interrupted dinners, forgotten birthdays, apologies and excuses and good intentions thwarted.

Traditionally, maintaining a family's social capital – the thousands of tiny emotional bonds and mutual niceties that tie us all together – was a wife's job. She would invite long-lost friends to supper, organise the children's play-dates, rustle up something for the fête and remember to feed the neighbours' cat. More seriously, she would also more often take responsibility for elderly parents, her own and often her husband's. And for middle-aged women, this kind of care is arguably becoming the new big feminist issue.

Women have a 50/50 chance of becoming carers by the time they're 59, when they are still probably working; men don't face the same odds until they are 75, when they may be physically frail but are no longer torn between love and work. The reason for this is that women tend to care for parents, who are usually the first to fall sick, and men tend to care much later on for their own spouses. 'This is a huge generalisation but men tend to care when there isn't a woman there to do it. They step in where they need to,' says Imelda Redmond, chief executive of Carers UK. Women do an unfair share of caring partly because they are likely to be working fewer hours (especially if they have already sidelined the career for the children) but also I suspect because they feel guiltier, more liable to be judged if they don't.

Guilt is not always a bad emotion, of course. It's what holds us steady within our complex web of social obligations, encouraging us to be better parents and friends (and more faithful lovers). But the trouble is, guilt is no more evenly shared than chores within couples. When Hewlett questioned her holders of 'extreme jobs' about the impact they felt their work had on their children, mothers were far quicker than fathers to blame themselves, fearing their work affected everything from their children's school performance to the amount of TV their children watched.[15] Mothers take every negative newspaper headline about working parents to heart, while fathers seem more able to let it wash over them.

Female guilt as well as male intransigence helps ensure men still do less domestic work (just over half as much as women)[16] or childcare. Guilt makes it harder to let go: it redoubles the working mother's desire to do 'better', and somehow manage the very things she no longer has time for. As the comedian Victoria Wood, the mother of two grown-up children, put it following the end of her 26-year marriage: 'I think I put myself under a lot of pressure to be a very present mother, and a very big comedian, and to be sort of running the household. So there was a lot to do, and it's difficult to keep everything in balance, and I was always tired, short of sleep, resentful. You could be onstage but you've got to come home and make a costume for a school play – and I think I took it all too seriously.'[17]

To ask why her then husband, a magician with a significantly less high profile career, couldn't make the costumes is missing the point: for mothers who feel like this, asking a man to pick up the slack is an admission of failure. They want to be able to do it all themselves. 'I do think men with working wives might get a raw deal on how tired and grumpy they are, but they get a good deal on the weekends,' says Olivia. 'I couldn't wait to be with my son at the weekends, couldn't wait to get up at 6 a.m.' Her full-time mother friends, meanwhile, happily hand over to their husbands on a Sunday morning.

Studies of how mothers spend their time repeatedly find working mothers making Herculean attempts to catch up on what they feel they've missed. One study at the University of Texas found that full-time mothers spent around two and a half hours a day purely interacting with their children – that is, not simultaneously doing something else while the children played – while working mothers spent only an hour less. At the weekends, the housewives spent just two hours a day interacting while the working mothers spent three.

The trouble is that mothers who run themselves ragged like this leave surprisingly little space for the father – and almost no energy for the overarching relationship that binds families together: the love affair, or what's left of it, with their partners.

The strange disappearance of sex in long-term relationships became such a common theme in letters to *The Times*'s sex columnist Suzi Godson that last year she embarked on her own survey of what was happening between the marital sheets. Not much, it seems: her initial findings were that the majority of British couples appeared to be having sex only once a month on a Saturday night.[18] Denise Hall, too, says working couples regularly come to Relate 'too tired, or not connected enough' for sex, and it's not just the women: Relate has recorded a 40 per cent increase in men complaining that they've gone off sex over the last decade.

In some households, the sexual desert is almost certainly created by silent mutual consent.

Yet in others, abstinence steals up through a marriage like rising damp, an unwanted and shameful chill in the air that neither partner quite knows how to cure. The exhausting days and broken nights that accompany small children are certainly not aphrodisiacs, but when newly formed couples can find the energy to stay up all night, tiredness seems an oddly unsatisfactory explanation for what is going on here. Could 'too tired' for sex translate more accurately sometimes as too angry?

Women in their thirties and forties certainly have time to project the illusion of sex, if not the reality: they kick hard against the invisibility that was once the lot of their own mothers, defending their right still to be regarded as glamorous sexual beings (although not necessarily always by their own partners). A quick glance around any baby swimming class suggests most mothers have time to paint their toenails without smudging once a week, which takes about as long as the average long-term married quickie. Yet the latter often slips out of the diary.

A booming industry has sprung up around this supposed crisis in female desire, flogging anything from hotel mini-breaks to designer bras and libido-boosting herbal supplements. Meanwhile the pharmaceutical industry devotedly pursues the concept of 'pink Viagra', the currently elusive pill to 'cure' low female sex drive. But drugs seem an alarmingly draconian and expensive solution when, according to one Australian study of working mothers, what's really killing female libido is at least partly suppressed anger over the unfair distribution of household chores.[19] Interestingly, in an American survey of sexless marriages conducted by Bob Berkowitz and his wife Susan Yager-Berkowitz almost half of the men said they had lost interest because they were angry: they resented being nagged and criticised by their wives.[20] The conventional excuses of time and tiredness were much further down the list of passion-killers. Could women's festering resentment, and men's anger at being nagged, represent two sides of the same domestic coin?

If the supposed epidemic of sexlessness were partly caused by an angry stand-off over the domestic workload, it would stand to reason that men who help more (and are presumably thus nagged less) should be having more sex. Oddly enough, research by the US marital therapist John Gottman bears that out.[21] In the modern marital economy, it's more than time and money that are being traded: the common currency most easily withheld when either side feels angry or hard done by is sex.

Men don't have to understand exactly why housework matters so much to their partners in order to see why it should matter to them. They simply need to know that they are paying an astonishingly high price for wriggling out of the dirty work at home. Not doing their fair share can mean family income lost, if an exhausted wife decides to quit or drastically reduce her hours rather than do everything; it can mean sex withheld, if she decides to do everything but that. But it can also threaten the security of their relationship with their children.

Women have now woken up to what the American journalist Leslie Bennetts calls the 'feminine mistake' – giving up work for motherhood as they are culturally conditioned to do, only to find they are helpless to provide for themselves if the marriage fails. But the evidence linking housework, sex and marital happiness suggests some men are making an equally big masculine mistake. By dodging domestic duties, they are both making divorce more likely and potentially writing themselves out of the family picture.

Before divorce was legalised in the UK in 1857, custody of children in a separation was usually given to the father, which meant women had the most to lose from marital breakdown. And even when maternal custody became common, a woman's lower earning power was a powerful deterrent to divorce. But in an age of both maternal custody and well-paid jobs for women, the uninvolved father now takes an enormous gamble: to disappear from your children's lives most of the time, even if it is to work, will hardly help you get a residence order if the marriage founders. Men are still culturally conditioned to secure their place in a family by providing for it, investing everything in work when they become fathers: but now that women are providers too, it's a terribly risky strategy. And I think deep down men are starting to realise that. There's a reason so many men say they are not happy with the balance between their work and home lives now, and that they would ideally like to share both the childcare and the burden of earning a living more equally: many are no happier with the tense state of their marriage than women are. And they may be starting to glimpse the opportunities that come with change.

Just as a tide going out uncovers the sand that was hidden beneath, job losses during the recession have exposed the way money and power were already shifting within families. Men lost their jobs much faster than women during the first wave, as male-dominated industries like the City and construction bore the brunt of redundancies, helping create a crucial tipping point for the traditional idea of the male breadwinner. By 2009, in Canada and Japan there were actually more women than men in work, with America on the brink of the same psychologically important transition. In Britain, women now earn either as much as, or more than, their partners in 44 per cent of couples.[22]

The playing field will probably level off somewhat now female jobs are being shed from the public sector, but the economy stumbling from the wreckage still looks surprisingly feminised: working hours down, flexibility up, girls emerging from school and university with better grades than boys and presumably better prospects, confirmed by the fact that young women now earn on average slightly more than young men. We are almost certainly about to see what happens when a critical mass of young women enter motherhood earning more than their children's fathers, reversing a traditional pattern where most women married men who earned more than them – almost guaranteeing that when they had children, it would be their careers that went on the back burner. If a £100,000 a year banker starts a family with a £20,000 nurse, it's not hard to guess who is likely to end up going part-time – but what if she's the banker, and he's the nurse? Four in ten young women now say they think in future it will be who earns most rather than gender that determines whose career takes precedence in a couple.[23] And in three years' time, they will have an unparalleled opportunity to put that theory into practice.

From 2015, fathers as well as mothers will be able to take substantial amounts of time off after a new baby's birth under government proposals for transferable parental leave. The first 18 weeks will be reserved for mothers recovering from the birth, but the rest of the year's leave can then be taken by either parent, or both together (with a 'daddy month' reserved for men, following evidence from Sweden and Iceland that men take leave only if some of it is specifically earmarked for them). It's a brave move that allows both parents to be involved from the start: interestingly, in two cases I found while researching this book of couples who had already managed to take several months off together with the baby, it wasn't the mother but her partner (the lower earner) who ended up spending more time at home in the long term.

Nonetheless, the predicted take-up of split leave by fathers remains pitifully low, and not only because it's badly paid: unless couples are wealthy enough both to stop work together, a man can only stay home if his partner is willing to surrender the baby. Everything rests, in the end, on how couples react to their changing circumstances.

For men, these economic and social changes are potentially painful, upending the balance of power in the home; for some women too, they mean difficult choices. But they are potentially a means of male *and* female liberation. By earning good money in their own right, women have begun to free their partners from the anxieties and the pressure of being sole breadwinners, giving them space to rethink their own careers. Men whose wives also earn have a new freedom not to chase the money but to chase the dream: to think about what they would like to do with their working lives, rather than what they have to do to pay the mortgage – and sometimes to take advantage of new working patterns originally pioneered by working mothers.

Stephen Overell of the Work Foundation identifies an interest in 'meaningful work' – a job that's not just about a pay cheque but is fulfilling and enjoyable, something that matches your values and engages your interest – as a coming trend in working life, one which he argues has been quietly building up for years. 'There's no mood for that in the current economic climate but in a year or two I suspect it will resurrect itself with the recovery. There's a sense that work is more important to people, that people have higher expectations of it. It matters in a way that is beyond simple income.'

Overell sees it as a logical consequence of the growing preoccupation with individual happiness and well-being. But it also strikes me as a feminisation of work: traditionally, men prioritise status and salary when choosing a career while women emphasise doing something that matches their values and makes them happy. Starting to think about work in this way can make for a different career trajectory, and also a very different balance between work and play – and perhaps, a subtly different relationship between men and women too. Everything points to change.

5

HALF A WIFE

A couple of months before my son was born, we moved across London into the tall, sunny Victorian terrace that was to be our family home. When my husband hacked back the overgrown shrubs in the garden, the old plum tree smothered beneath them burst first into candyfloss blossom and then rather feebly into fruit. That summer, while the baby slept in his Moses basket and Gordon Brown embarked on a political honeymoon I should otherwise have been covering, I stayed home and made pots of purple jam with gingham-checked lids. Nothing could have been further removed from my normal life, and my husband was as amused as I was faintly embarrassed by it all. But I remember that summer like the mythical summers of childhood, sunny and sweet: although in reality doubtless it was as wet as it ever is, and sleepless too.

The next August, after a bit of judicious watering, the plum tree was even more laden. I made jam again, perhaps hoping to recapture something of the summer before, but that something was gone. After six months back at work, I was still struggling to prove myself on every front: I ended up stubbornly stoning mountains of plums at midnight, knife slipping with tiredness, no longer enjoying it but refusing to concede defeat. Stopping would have been an admission that it wasn't possible to live both lives; that the desire to write and think and influence could not be reconciled with a subterranean desire, emerging only after motherhood, to make and create and nurture. The year after that, I didn't have time to thin the tree out in spring and by late July it was so over-laden with fruit that half the trunk sheared off beneath the weight. But by then, the house was already on the market and I was mentally composing my resignation letter. That November, we moved out of the city to rural Oxfordshire and I began a new phase of my career, writing freelance from home.

I didn't give up a great job to make jam. But I gave it up, as an awful lot of parents do, because while my identity was no longer defined by work alone, my days all too often were. I wanted to preserve a life in more than one narrow dimension – to be able to keep one foot at home and one in interesting work, instead of scrabbling frantically for toeholds in both. And it wasn't just my life that changed as a result.

We soon realised that if I was no longer tied to working in the House of Commons, but could work from home, then my husband's long-held desire to live in the country rather than the city was suddenly within reach. We were no longer locked into that crazy cycle which always reminds me of the nursery rhyme about the little old lady who swallowed the fly: having to do certain jobs in order to earn the money that paid the mortgage on the house we bought mostly so that we were, ahem, near enough the office to do those jobs.

Living in the country isn't all roses around the door and chickens in the garden. There are times when I miss not just old friends but some metropolitan grit in the oyster: the crowds, the buzz, the West End theatres and East End gigs which made me feel vaguely cultured by association (even though we were mostly too tired to actually go to them). But I don't miss the crazed competition over half-decent schools or the knifepoint muggings on our doorstep. My son has a freedom here I wouldn't have dared give him in London, and walking the dog across the rolling downs in late summer, through hedgerows dripping with blackberries and rosehips, has its own compensations. Then there is the fact that although I make the trip to London every few weeks for meetings, or just for a change of scene, these days my morning journey to work consists mostly of wandering downstairs to make a cup of coffee. This summer, my 'office' has as often as not been a laptop on the garden table, at which I sometimes wonder whether wi-fi will end up liberating almost as many women as the Pill.

Many parents who work two or three or four days a week talk about having time just 'to be a parent', or at least the kind of parent they want to be. For others, it's about feeling that full-time would be too much, and not working too little: part-time is an acceptable compromise. But working in unconventional patterns (by which I mean anything other than standard office hours, five days a week) is surely also about riding out the contradictions in wanting to be with one's children yet part of something bigger too; for me it's about being able, in the words of Walt Whitman, to contain multitudes. Working for three days a week and mothering for two feels, to me, rather like living in a small child's Etch a Sketch. The working days fill with frantic scribble: the morning rush to get everyone out of the house, then long intense hours of writing, followed by a crunching gear change and the rush of collecting my son from childminder or preschool, then supper, bath and bed. On the mothering days, the screen is wiped blank again: we potter about, make a mess, chat. These days don't run to the steady linear rhythm of work but exist in that strange toddler vortex where time goes backwards, forwards and sideways – and then round and round in circles, minutely examining an ant. There are clean sheets, coffees with friends, time to notice the weather – and the next day, more frantic scribbling. It's a way of keeping multiple identities alive: and that is what I came to think of as being half a wife, but holding on to at least half a life – since personally speaking, I couldn't imagine a life without work.

Just as workaholics need to switch off from the office at least for a few hours a week, even the happiest homemaker needs to have some small time to call their own beyond the domestic sphere – a few hours a week just to stretch the mind and play some part in the workings of the wider world. That might mean paid work, or study, or volunteering, or pursuing another passion entirely; but all of us deserve some private mental space. So by 'half a wife', I simply mean the role that is necessary to the smooth running of a home and family: and by 'half a life', I mean that which is necessary to one's own sanity. And for me, it was the former that initially seemed hardest to pin down.

What does it mean in the 21st century, to be a wife? Surely not what it did forty years ago, when in a bleakly satirical essay for *Ms* magazine entitled 'I want a wife', the writer Judy Syfers detailed all the reasons why men might want a spouse. The 'wife' she depicts is an obedient servant, a dumb helpmeet who must honour and obey the husband, the children – and even the home. 'I want a wife who will take care of my physical needs. I want a wife who will keep my house clean. A wife who will pick up after my children, a wife who will pick up after me,' wrote Syfers. 'I want a wife to go along when our family takes a vacation so that someone can continue to care for me and my children when I need a rest and a change of scene.' Who wouldn't want a wife like this? she concludes. But very few of us would now aspire to *be* her.

The modern working wife has briskly outsourced much of the work Syfers described to an array of paid helpers – cleaners, childminders, online supermarket delivery drivers – and arguably unpaid ones too. It's the grandparents now who often 'go along when our family takes a vacation' to babysit, and who somewhat heroically fill in the gaps in many overstretched working families. But there is a part of being a 'wife' that was always more than glorified skivvy, and that's the part we are still struggling with.

This is the wife as collective memory, repository of The Knowledge – that exhaustive domestic map of exactly what needs doing when and by whom, which is necessary before you can make anyone help you do it: the wife who manages the family's social capital and its emotional health. It's wife as air traffic controller, tracking the erratic flight paths of the family through domestic space – who needs swimming kit on Thursday, which child has inexplicably fallen out with their best friend, how long it is since anyone rang the in-laws. This wife is the architect of the family's relationship to the outside world, she who both knows where the Sellotape is and remembered the birthday in the first place. And this is what dual earner couples are really talking about when they sigh that what they both really need is a wife. 'I just want somebody else to deal with all that "what have we bought my mother for her birthday" or "when are we seeing my sister again" or "when are the So-and-Sos coming round" – because these things magically happen, apparently,' says Liz, a voluntary sector executive.

What constitutes this kind of 'wife work' is an entirely personal thing, although in this house this week it's included the normal household chores plus tracking down a Spiderman costume for one of those compulsory children's fancy dress days apparently

designed to catch parents out; ordering a wedding present; a trip
to the vet; a morning at the village school my son will soon be
attending; booking a hotel for a weekend away; and working out
how to kill the ants' nest under the kitchen floorboards without
poisoning the dog too. But for me at least, being a 'wife' in this
sense isn't really a full-time job (unlike being a parent, which is
a 24/7 state of mind whether you are with your children or not).
When I sat down to work out how much time we needed to
restore some kind of sanity to family life, I reckoned we only
really needed about two days' worth of 'wife time' carved out of
a working week, both to cram in chores and to restore the parental
time with my son that felt so sorely missing, while giving us all
room to breathe. (Sheer exhaustion, and the panicky state of
burnout that accompanies it, is a seriously underrated factor in
many parents' decisions to shorten their hours.) We didn't really
need a full-time wife: we only needed half of her.

The great thing about being at home two days a week is that
it feels, at its best, like pulling off a conjuring trick: you are
magically more present than absent both at work and at home,
since you're in the office for three out of five working days, yet
still with the children for four out of seven days. Both sides have
more than half of you (although never enough of you). No wonder
so many British couples choose to solve the domestic dilemma
by one parent going down to a two- or three-day working week,
leaving them with roughly one and a half earners plus half a
wife. It's the pattern my own family life most closely matches,
and it can be the happiest solution for all concerned, depending
on the careers and circumstances of each parent.

But the 'one and a half earner' pattern is also the one couples
can fall into without really thinking, just because it's the easiest.
Her boss has probably vaguely expected a request for reduced
hours ever since she got pregnant – it's easier to shorten her hours

if she earns less, and if she's already spent a year with the children on maternity leave she is probably the more emotionally entangled parent. She may see the issue largely as one of how long she can bear to be away from the children: he may retreat, regarding the whole mess – whether with relief or with sadness – as not his business. But since we know that only about a quarter of men would work full-time if money were no object, this 'one and a half earner' model may well be what fathers are resigned to getting, rather than what they ideally want.

When the pollsters YouGov asked in a 2009 survey whether a mother of primary school children should work part-time, full-time or not at all if she could afford it, the popular vote was for part-time work, just as it is in real life. But like countless other polls crossing my desk with wearying regularity, it only asked what the *mother* should do; it's just assumed that the father carries on working all hours regardless. There's no box to tick if you think perhaps her husband should consider changing his job too. As in polling, so often in corporate culture, policy-making and law too: the question of what a father might do when a dual career couple feels stretched too thin isn't even asked, so the sadness and the guilt and the problem to be solved is all laid at her door. And we should be very careful about where that leads us.

Perhaps the most obvious example of what happens when women abandon conventional working patterns en masse lies in the Netherlands, where the 'one and a half earner' pattern is endemic. Three in four Dutch women work shortened hours, and part-time is a perfectly normal choice even for women without children (or with grown-up children). That reflects a culture which, for all the familiar stereotypes of legalised dope smoking and frank sexuality, is actually surprisingly conservative, with a strongly embedded belief that children are best raised by their parents (not in nurseries) and that it's a woman's job to look after the home.

The majority of Dutch women seem happy with a deal that ensures plenty of free time, while the part-time wife is a 'clear favourite' with Dutch men, according to research from the Netherlands Institute of Social Research.[1] Women can, and do, work a three-day week even at senior levels (although they may not quite reach the top of the tree). Despite this, the Dutch government has recently established a task force on persuading women to work more hours, and for good reason. When very short hours become a permanent lifestyle choice for women of all ages, they may fail to earn and save enough for retirement and the economy may grow more slowly. The feminist critique, meanwhile, of a life spent hanging out agreeably in cafés is that women are being suckered into a risky financial dependency on men – and girls are being raised to think it isn't normal for a woman to have a full-blown career.

The Dutch example isn't a reason to reject the 'one and a half' earner pattern. But it is definitely a red flag, a warning that if half a wife always equals half a woman, then women may well find themselves pulled backwards. And so what separates the half a wife this book describes from Syfers's poor downtrodden wife is that 'she' could as easily be a 'he', and better still a 'they': a couple shouldering half of the job once done by an old-fashioned housewife.

Grandparents or siblings or some other combination of loving adults could also provide at least part of these two days' grace in some families. Well-off and guilt-free dual earner couples can buy in some 'wife time': unlike a nursery, a nanny will wait in for the repairman and make the World Book Day costume, although someone still has to deal with the intimate leftovers of life. 'Wife time' could also be painstakingly stitched together from scraps: two hours a day here gained by him working from home sometimes instead of commuting, or her taking the odd afternoon off because she's freelance. Even divorced couples can still split the school run if they remain on friendly terms. There are dozens of ways in which families can share the 'wife work' while still ensuring that each member hangs on to half a life. But they require a mental leap that many of us still don't take.

Surprisingly few of the mothers I interviewed about quitting full-time jobs had seriously explored the idea of their husband cutting his working hours instead. Perhaps in many cases they didn't ask because they knew their partners weren't interested; but that doesn't quite explain the domino effect visible in some couples where, after watching their wives happily launching more laid-back careers, the husbands also became restless. I have to admit that, over a year of trying to work out what was wrong with our family life, I can't remember ever seriously asking my husband if he wanted not to be the breadwinner. Was I worried he might say yes?

There are sacrifices involved in a more egalitarian family life, and for women the big one is having to leave the safety of the maternal high ground – the assumption that mothers are essentially more important to children than fathers, which so often springs from a fear that mothering is what we will ultimately be judged upon, mingled with a fear of missing out on our children. Maternal gatekeeping is a hidden barrier not just to the fair division of housework but often to the fair division of time with the children, and ultimately of work: what stands between a family and a half a wife arrangement may be the female fantasy of being the whole wife, while simultaneously juggling a blissful marriage and epic full-time career. But the rewards of sharing work and care between a couple can be substantial. The happiest couples, in a landmark 2011 study by the campaign group Working Families, were not men with partners working part-time but those who were both full-time, yet critically both had some flexibility.[2]

Men were also happier when they did more housework, in keeping with Wendy Sigle-Rushton's findings. 'You can read that as just being that once your wife's full time you have got more money, but taken with the housework finding, there does seem to be something about couples liking to feel they are equal,' says Sarah Jackson, of Working Families. These men have managed to avoid the masculine mistake of becoming semi-detached from their home lives, and are reaping the benefits. Family life may be not just fairest but happiest when both sexes can have satisfying work if they want it, but also sometimes read the bedtime story or hang out at the school gate – for their own benefit, and for their children's.

When asked what exactly they would do with their children if given more time, both sexes put 'more days out' at the top of the list, and both want to do more of the school runs.[3] After that, men would play more, do more sport, and help more with homework. Women would bake more, play more, and do more crafts. Fathers, if given more time, would use it differently than mothers – and the result would be richer lives for children.

This is no criticism of single or same-sex parents, who usually make sterling efforts to round out their children's lives. But where there is both a mother and a father in a home, the evidence supports engaging both in childcare. One reason that the children of lesbian parents do better academically, have higher self-esteem and fewer behavioural problems than straight couples' children,[4] according to an American study which followed children through to their teens, is that both parents tend to be heavily involved in their children's lives and back each other up. Children in a two-parent family who don't spend time with both parents may miss something specific.

A doting full-time working father can, of course, still put in this time with his children at weekends; but as full-time working

mothers could tell them, that doesn't leave much time to recover
before Monday rolls around again. Even in the Netherlands, there
are signs that the 'one and a half earner' model may be a stepping
stone towards a more radical split of work and care within families.

According to recent research by the sociologists Fritz van Wel
and Trudie Knijn,[5] a third of Dutch women now say they would
ideally prefer both themselves and their partners to work reduced
hours, allowing them to split work and care more evenly between
them. (The main obstacle, Wel and Knijn concluded, was that
'for the time being, they have not succeeded in persuading their
partner to work part-time'. As we've seen, their partners may well
fear the competitive consequences.) But one in ten Dutch couples
do now both work shortened hours, and among professional
couples in particular, there is a growing preference for both to
work a four-day week (potentially needing only three days'
childcare, if they each take a different day off). The hidden
advantage of this 'Four by Four' model is that it matches what
employers seem to want.

There is a huge unspoken difference in many professional
employers' minds between four days – regarded as still being just
about in the game – and anything less. 'People will say "Four
days isn't really part time, is it?"' says Karen Mattison, co-founder
of the social enterprise Women Like Us, which matches parents
with part-time work. 'I'd say yes, and part-time can be anything,
but it automatically conjures up "only till three o'clock" or "only
three days". That one day more can make an unbelievable amount
of difference.'

For mothers of young children in particular, cutting out just
one working day a week often barely feels worth it: it has all the
professional downside of going part-time, without much reducing
the time children spend in daycare or lightening the load at home.
But abandoning the assumption that the two days' 'wife time'

must all come from a mother, and asking how your child can have another two days *with one or other of his parent*s rather than always the same one, can change the picture completely. My hunch is that four-day weeks for mothers, with all their professional advantages, will become far more desirable if four-day weeks for fathers also catch on.

Yet another way of sharing work and care is to do it consecutively, with the parents taking time out at different stages of their lives and swapping roles over the years. For example, a woman might take the first year off with the baby, then go back to work full-time while her partner becomes a househusband; later on, they may swap again. This 'consecutive wife' model works best for couples where one or both work in a trade that is relatively easy to pick up and put down again, from cab driving to acting – although as we'll see in the following chapters, with an imaginative employer the 'consecutive wife' model can work even in the most traditional of careers.

For parents of older children, another trick is to carve out lengthy periods of family time in between work projects: 'wife time' could be a single block of three months a year between contracts, rather than two days a week. Hilary Sears is chair of Interim Women, a network set up for female interim managers – experienced managers who can be hired either to cover temporary gaps in companies, such as maternity leave, or to troubleshoot specific time-limited projects. Interims typically work in six-month bursts and often seek to take time off in between, which is one way of combining absorbing work with periods of re-immersion in family life.

Sears describes a colleague who has just embarked on an interim posting: 'She had just had three months at home after coming out of a full-time job in a bank, which was fantastic because her daughter was doing AS levels and she was able to spend time with her and get to know her daughter again. She's now working flat out again but she knows it will only be for six months.' Interims tend to be in their fifties, so often have teenage children who don't need their parents hovering daily but do sometimes want more intensive attention.

Interim managers are also, of course, usually sufficiently well paid to be able to afford chunks of time off between jobs. But what about the many thousands of working parents who are not so lucky?

There is no point pretending that fewer hours worked doesn't often mean less money in the bank, at a time when there are more mouths to feed. For families already on the edge financially, that simply doesn't add up – which is why, in coming chapters, we'll look at imaginative ways the state could help ease the financial pressures on half a wife families. Even for higher earners, there are painful choices to be made. Getting one's life back can mean learning to live with new anxieties about money in exchange for reducing old ones about time. 'I could have been living in a house with land around it, and driving a 4x4 imperiously round the country lanes, instead of living in a semi and driving an old Golf,' as Vicky, the former banker, puts it. While she still feels that having a more relaxed family life 'makes up for not staying in so many nice hotels', those who recoil from similar sacrifices should ask themselves how much they really want more time – or whether they would really rather buy it in from nannies, cleaners and other professional services.

Despite all of this, the relationship between time and money isn't always as obvious as it seems. My theories about this were put to the ultimate test when a little over a year after I quit, my husband's job – he was by now working locally in Oxfordshire – came under threat. After years in which we both earned much the same, he was now the main breadwinner; and I knew I couldn't support us on my now smaller earnings, despite having downshifted to a cheaper life in the country. The nice, safe job I threw away had never looked so desirable.

But it didn't take long to see that the smug security of our dual-earning years had been an illusion. Like so many of our friends, we began family life with a London mortgage that needed both salaries to pay it: I couldn't have covered that mortgage on my own even at the peak of my earnings. And while as a full-timer I had almost no scope to bump up my earnings in a rocky patch, a three-day freelance week can become five days in a crisis. Changing the way they use time can leave couples poorer on paper but in some ways more financially resilient, at least to short-lived shocks. And when I did the sums, it became clear that what we had lost in salary by my giving up full-time office-based work, we saved almost to the penny in cheaper childcare (a childminder instead of a nanny, for three shorter days a week) and lower housing costs outside London.

The hidden costs of working – childcare, housing, travel – mean there are models of downshifting that already make surprisingly good economic sense at both the top and the bottom of the income scale. For low to middling earners who feel strongly that their children should be brought up within the family rather than using paid childcare, a 'swinging door' lifestyle where both parents work two or three days a week – but never at the same time – can work well. The saving on nursery bills means that, if they qualify for tax credits as low earners, 'swinging door' couples could earn almost as much as they might working full-time. A teacher earning £30,000 married to a police sergeant earning £35,000 with two children in nursery full-time, for example, may end up only marginally worse off if she works two days and he works three than if they both worked full-time. They save on childcare, and receive extra tax credits.

'Swinging door' couples may work as little as five days between them, the same as a traditional breadwinner married to a traditional homemaker, instead of the eight days they could manage under a half a wife arrangement. But as they have both kept some kind of work ticking over rather than having a complete break, they may still find it easier than full-time homemakers to get back into the game when their children are older. With childcare bills now rising steeply above inflation and salaries flatlining, 'swinging door' families could become increasingly common.

For some wealthier families, meanwhile, 2013 brings an unexpected one-off opportunity to cut their hours without losing out financially, thanks to the scrapping of child benefit for any family where someone pays higher rate tax. If you're only just over the threshold to start with, negotiating slightly reduced hours – say, a Friday afternoon off – could push your salary back below the higher rate, which means the family holds on to their child benefit. For families with three or more children in particular, the deal may end up effectively paying for itself, giving them a free afternoon with the children at the Chancellor's expense. But for both high and low earning families, there is one really ingenious trick for clawing back time without losing money. It simply requires thinking less like a working mother, and more like a man.

Men are almost half as likely as women to say they would like to work part-time in their current job.[6] It's not that they don't want more time, but they are far warier than women of sacrificing salary and status for it. 'Men aren't stupid. They look around and see what happens to women and they make a very direct connection: "She was doing fine, now she's had a baby and now look – why would I want to expose myself to that risk?"' says Sarah Jackson of Working Families. When presented with a list of flexible working options, men are more likely than women to favour working from home; working compressed hours (cramming five days' work into four, but still being paid for five); and working annualised hours, where employers require a set number of hours over the year but workers can be sent home at slack times and do unpaid overtime at peak periods.[7] Oddly enough, none of these options are necessarily unacceptable at senior levels and none involves losing a penny of earned income. (Compressed working can even leave parents better off, if they currently have full-time childcare: they save on a day's nursery bills but keep the same salary.)

In other words, men are drawn towards flexible working styles that don't make them feel they have failed as providers. A man who works like this can actually think of himself as having got one over on the boss, scoring more time without surrendering salary. The idea of ripping through five days' work in only four may also appeal to macho pride. Are women selling themselves short by so often choosing to work part-time, rather than holding out for one of the full-pay options?

Compressed working doesn't suit anyone worried about spending long days apart from a baby, or determined to be at the school gates every day. But home working for at least some of the week might, if it's in the kind of job where you can work short but intense days, finishing off when the children are in bed. Parents of school-aged children in particular are missing a trick if they don't consider the full-pay options. There is just one snag, and it's a big one: the three full-pay options are currently the three least commonly offered kinds of flexible working in the UK. Arguably, what stops many families moving towards the half a wife model is that it's genuinely harder for men (and increasingly for high-earning, or sole-breadwinning, women) to find the flexible jobs they want; namely, jobs compatible either with actually being a 'provider', or with *feeling* like one. But if men's working habits remain fixed in stone, then women's choices will inevitably remain limited.

So while some readers will by now have seen how they could move towards a half a wife lifestyle, for others it will still seem tantalisingly out of reach. And what that shows us is that parents cannot ultimately do this on their own: if the half a wife model is to reach its full potential, employers – and ultimately governments – will need to make changes too.

In the coming chapters, we'll explore a series of practical and realistic changes that could be made at all levels of national life, which between them would allow both mothers and fathers more of the time they need. We'll look at new trends in working life – from demographic change to the hidden costs of keeping people in an office – which open up the possibilities for parents. We'll look at what innovative companies are doing already to unpick conventional working patterns, and at the unexpected benefits for them of doing so: and at what more governments could do both to encourage them, and to support families in their daily lives.

However tight the public purse strings, I still think it's both morally and economically right for the state to subsidise childcare for moderate earners. There will always be a yawning gap between what parents can afford from their taxed salaries and what good childcare costs, and if it isn't filled, some will have no choice but to give up work. That's not just sad, but unbelievably expensive, once you tot up the taxes they'll no longer pay and the benefits they may well claim instead. For that reason, last year's incredibly short-sighted cuts to childcare tax credit should be reversed. But there are limits on what parents can realistically expect other taxpayers to bear.

There's no denying it would all be easier with tax-free childcare, or parental leave paid at 90 per cent of salary for a year, or any other magic bullet liable to cost billions: it would have been all too tempting to write a book demanding these things. But it would have been meaningless, since those are emphatically not the times in which we now live. It would cost just over £1 billion simply to extend the current (very) part-time free nursery places to all two-year-olds: and to put it bluntly, when the government is stripping profoundly disabled people of benefits and sacking war veterans, tax breaks for people with nannies aren't a popular priority. (Nor will this spending squeeze melt away any time soon – thanks to an ageing population, by 2050 we'll be spending an estimated fifth of our entire national wealth on services for the elderly. The tide of public money is shifting away from the cradle, much closer to the grave.)

But that doesn't mean all hope is lost. It simply means parents must become more imaginative in their demands, more ruthless at prioritising, and smarter at exploiting changes already happening beneath the surface of working life. And in return for help where they need it, parents must also be honest about the extent to which domestic choices shape working ones: which means those who think their problem lies in the office need first to check that it doesn't actually lie rather closer to home. If you are burning out mostly (or even partly) because you are working 50 hours a week and your partner does next to nothing around the house, then that is not your employer's fault but your spouse's. The journey towards a half a wife family starts, quite literally, by putting your own house in order.

6

RETHINKING FAMILY LIFE

As a working mother of five-year-old twin boys, Lisa understandably has a lot on her plate. But the one thing she doesn't really have to worry about is what happens at home. She and her partner divide domestic duties so scrupulously fairly that when I ask both of them what they think it would be like if one of them did nothing around the house, they are puzzled. 'How it works is that one of us would not want to see the other one struggle,' Lisa eventually explains. 'We're just kind to each other. It's about not assuming.'

Lisa, a scenic artist, spent the first year at home with the twins but her partner was careful to be home in the mornings and evenings in time to see the boys. Who does the school run now is determined by who's working closest, and they both work four days a week, sharing the 'wife time' between them. What's the secret of this enviable domestic bargain? Simple: Lisa's partner is another woman. And like many gay families, they offer straight couples a fascinating insight into what happens to family life if you strip out stereotypical ideas of what mothers and fathers are 'supposed' to do and simply go back to the drawing board.

Because they can't fall unthinkingly into traditional parenting roles, gay parents have to devise a role for the birth parent and for the other partner from scratch. That's why I asked a gay parents' group in southern England if they would kindly distribute to their members a questionnaire for me on how family life is organised.

Scanning the results quickly put paid to any assumption that two women would gladly share chores because they're both somehow 'hard-wired' for domesticity: even the woman who noted acidly on her questionnaire that 'housework bores me', and those who admitted they'd rather spend less time at home, still dutifully tried to share the chores fairly. Where the lesbian mothers I surveyed worked fewer hours than their partners, they usually did more hands-on childcare – cooking meals and changing nappies – because they were around more. But they split 'strategic mothering' tasks like deciding how to discipline the children, while the parent working more hours was (like Lisa's partner Catriona) usually anxious to help when she was home. They tended to share out domestic work according to ability rather than preconceived ideas about who was supposed to do what, with whoever was the more organised doing the bills and paperwork, and whoever was less ham-fisted doing the DIY. 'It's easier in some ways because there are no assumptions about who is going to be in charge of what,' as Lisa puts it. Perhaps unsurprisingly, several of the lesbian mothers I interviewed had straight friends, sisters or mothers who envied their relationships.

The fact that gay couples usually need to conceive by IVF may well be a factor: several of the couples I interviewed mentioned having had longer than usual to discuss how things would work, because they had to save up for treatment, and the non-birth parent may also have made such painstaking efforts to bond with their child in part because they weren't biologically related. They felt they had to 'work' at the relationship, in a way straight fathers sometimes don't.

But the overriding common factor was that when asked why

they arranged things the way they did, these couples tended to talk about emotions rather than practicalities: love and respect, consideration and fairness. Sally, a part-time lecturer, who has two sons aged one and four with her civil partner, was typical: 'I would hate Lorraine to feel she had to do everything and she would hate for me to feel I'm the only one who could possibly clean a toilet. We care for and love our family and all do as much as we can.' When two parents attach the same emotional value to housework, it can perhaps be traded more fairly, because they agree on what it's worth: there is a common exchange rate.

Similarly, gay fathers in one American study were found to share domestic duties and paid work more evenly, with both, for example, working a four-day week instead of having one parent at home. Researchers found that 'both partners made personal sacrifices, so that neither partner had more responsibility at home or less infringement on their work life than the other'.[1] In their free time, instead of creating a caretaker 'mummy' role and a more distant 'daddy' role, each did all the routine childcare tasks in turn. Gay fathers, interestingly, tend to say they're more satisfied with their home lives and their relationships generally than straight parents. As the researchers concluded, gay couples may have something to teach the rest of us, fumbling incoherently as we are towards a more equal kind of family life.

It is, of course, far easier said than done for straight couples to throw off the shackles of domestic stereotypes overnight. So I want to examine in this chapter how even relatively small changes in the way family life is organised – not just within couples, but more widely across the generations – could help us start to find the time we need. What is it that successful, close-knit families do to make each other's lives easier?

Even those with enviably egalitarian home lives tend to be either maddeningly vague about how it actually happens, or irritatingly glib about how easy it is to achieve. One couple I read about in an American time management manual boasted of having a whiteboard, on which they'd write things that needed doing around the house: when either had any spare time they would pick 'a bunch of things' off the board and do them. I know exactly how this would work in my house. I'd religiously write up the jobs, my husband would scrawl witticisms over them, and I'd end up resentfully crossing all the jobs off.

Such methods do offer transparency, since the unequal work record is right up there for everyone to see. But the man who overlooks a stack of dirty dishes can merrily ignore a whiteboard too, which means these methods are really reminders of chores to be done, not ways of determining who does them. (If the whiteboard couple are egalitarian enough to spend their spare time companionably ticking chores off, they're egalitarian enough not to need a whiteboard.) By contrast, many overburdened spouses simply stagger rather inconsistently on, periodically losing their temper but mostly putting up with it, sending hopelessly mixed messages and never quite confident enough in demanding change to achieve it.

My own unscientific gleanings over a year wrestling with the domestic deal boil down to five lessons for the put-upon spouse, who is statistically more likely to be, but isn't always, a woman.

First and foremost, the aggrieved spouse should examine honestly how much of the inequality is their fault. It can help to ask not 'How can I get my partner to do more?' but 'How did he get me to do more in the first place?' Sometimes, it's through bullying: sulking, shouting, making life so unpleasant when asked that the spouse doesn't ask again. Women in these marriages should consider professional counselling (and women intimidated into doing everything by violence or threats obviously need professional help). But often it's a more complicated business. Fewer fathers than mothers agree that it is a 'mum's job' to look after the home and children,[2] suggesting that men may dodge some domestic responsibilities but women may also fend them off, criticising, interfering, hovering and correcting whenever a man tries to help. It can pay handsomely to remember that men handle children differently to women, but not necessarily wrongly; and anyway, nobody died of having their Babygro on backwards. But for women who feel strongly that they're ultimately judged on their mothering and housekeeping abilities, delegating to a man can feel risky and threatening. What if he doesn't do it to her standards? Even worse, what if he does, and it turns out she is more dispensable than she thought?

When I sat down with a list of weekly domestic chores to work out which ones I actually wanted help with, the answers surprised me. Cooking? Oh, but I enjoy that. Food shopping? If I'm honest, I quite like that too. Cleaning the loo? That I wouldn't miss. But since it takes ten minutes a week, it's not the reason I feel exhausted. And childcare is even more of a minefield. I don't want always to be the one doing bath and bedtime, but I don't want to miss time with my son either. A couple of nights off a week would be fine. 'Fair' is sometimes not a 50/50 split but what both sides feel is fair, and what plays to both sides' strengths.

The second lesson is that maternal gatekeeping isn't to blame for everything: and that new fathers should be made more aware of the risks of making the masculine mistake. That means not just men being more alert to what is happening in their own marriages but women spelling out more clearly to their partners the consequences of failing to engage domestically, rather than festering in angry silence.

The third, and closely related, lesson is that 'it's not fair' is a remarkably weak argument for change. It may not be fair, but that's what toddlers and underlings say, and it only invites a long, meandering argument about fairness – whose job is harder, whether children are more stressful than the office, whether walking the dog genuinely equals cleaning the bathroom – which conveniently distracts from the task at hand. It is critical not to allow oneself to be distracted, and above all not to give up.

That doesn't mean daily nagging: better to take 15 minutes on a Sunday night to go through the diary for the week working out what needs doing, and who can do it. If it isn't done, grievances should if possible be stored for next Sunday. Domestically incompetent spouses may eventually learn that Sunday nights will be over faster if they do roughly what they were meant to. One reason many undomesticated spouses hate talking about housework is that it's to their advantage not to: if you stop talking about it, you will slip back into default mode again.

And the fourth lesson is to employ that other underused source of domestic labour: children. Three-quarters of secondary-school-aged children have never loaded a washing machine or cleaned a bathroom, according to a survey conducted by the Children's Society, which found that the majority of teenagers were simply no longer expected to do household chores.[3] Working parents may want their limited time at home to be fun, rather than a battle of wills, but not asking children to do chores actually does them no favours. Helping around the house teaches altruism, respect for others and unselfishness as well as basic life skills. School-aged children who do housework with their father are more likely to get along with their peers, and less likely to disobey teachers or make trouble at school, according to an analysis by sociologists Scott Coltrane and Michele Adams of the University of California, Riverside.[4] Even a two-year-old can pick up her own toys at the end of the day, while a three-year-old can lay the cutlery for dinner – if you don't mind some eccentric *placements* – and chuck his dirty clothes in the laundry. A seven-year-old can make her own bed, and secondary school children should be learning how to cook and serve a basic family meal.

Mothers of boys, I think, have a particular moral duty to their future daughters-in-law here. One morning, when my son was around three – the age at which toddlers begin beadily sorting the world by gender – I remember him watching me drag out the vacuum cleaner and asking doubtfully, 'Does Daddy know how to hoover?' What children see us do (and not do) sets the tone for the next generation of parenthood.

But the final lesson is one that often comes too late for parents. It's a lot easier to start all this before having children. Young women prone to swooning that their boyfriend will be 'a really great father' because he likes small children should learn to check instead how often he stacks the dishwasher, perhaps a better indicator of a man ready to share the routine daily work involved in family life. Antenatal preparation for couples, meanwhile, could usefully include slightly fewer charming but pointless breathing exercises, and more emphasis on discussing honestly how life changes after a baby, and who is going to do what. The Fatherhood Institute has recently won government funding for just such a pilot programme, based on an American scheme known as Family Foundation, which offers new parents antenatal and postnatal classes covering not just the practicalities of having a baby but an exploration of how relationships are likely to be affected. 'They'll talk about how most people argue a lot more, how what you do about that can save you from a real loss of relationship satisfaction,' says Rob Williams of the Fatherhood Institute. 'It's been really successful in helping couples stay together. There's much less risk of separating three years later' (among couples who complete the course).

Interestingly, the single most important quality I found in those couples who were sharing work and care more evenly was that they saw family life as a joint project, 'wife work' as a joint responsibility, and both careers as closely entwined. They were highly conscious of the impact their decisions had on each other, rather than competing with each other, and that made it possible for them to approach work in a very different way. Most strikingly, the fathers tended to be good at seeing success in terms of the whole family's happiness, rather than just their own professional status.

Tim and Julia have two small children aged three and five, and when we spoke were both working four days a week, with each having a day of 'wife time' at home. He set up his own PR consultancy after their second child was born, while she works at a senior level in corporate public affairs, where four days is about as part-time as she could get away with. She has Fridays with the children while he takes Mondays, 'bookending' the children's week so that they only need childcare for three days.

They hit on this 'four by four' solution after their second child was diagnosed with the feeding disorder reflux. As his wife struggled to cope with a toddler and a constantly vomiting baby, Tim was inevitably drafted in more. 'He wasn't an easy baby, and my memories of the first month were basically of burned fingers in the middle of the night, endlessly sterilising things in hot water when I was half asleep. He just wasn't taking any milk in. So I was really involved with him right from the start and because it was quite heavy going, that started the thought process about work,' he recalls. Six months later, Tim quit to start his own business.

Around the same time Julia, who was still on maternity leave, landed a new job with a different company and managed to negotiate a four-day week – which made Tim in turn think harder about what he now wanted to do with his time. 'It seemed only fair that I did four days as well – and anyway, I wanted to do it,' he says.

It wasn't always plain sailing. Tim found it hard to limit his hours while getting the business off the ground, and decided early on to keep quiet about his day at home in case it spooked his clients. 'I probably only told one client I didn't work on Mondays. With the others I worked around it: if one of them was saying "I need you to write something today" I'd say "I'm busy all day but I can do something tomorrow or this evening." It's different if you work for yourself: people always assume that you're busier than you are.'

Tim might well have earned more by staying in his old job, but without his domestic support, Julia might have been pushed into a more junior and less well paid role. Overall, he has no regrets: 'I feel that's time I have forever got in the bank with the children, that I benefited from and they will always have benefited from. I know what goes in their lunchboxes, I know how they feel about things, I know what they do in the day. I know how good at climbing up or down things they are,' he says.

'It's stuff you can pick up on a bit at weekends, but you have a different dynamic when it's just you and them. One of you will take more of a back seat when you're both there.' What comes across strongly is the sense that they are both in it together. Since at first Julia's hours were more fixed, Tim did the cooking and the laundry; cleaning duties are determined by 'who's around, rather than any gender thing'.

But it isn't just give and take within their marriage that makes Tim and Julia's family life possible: it's give and take within their extended family. The middle three days when both are working are mostly covered by school and preschool, but Tim is frank that they wouldn't have managed without the help of both grandparents and Tim's brother, a teacher, who often helps out after school. Their half a wife is arguably a whole family effort, and one that spans at least two generations.

A quarter of British working parents, and half of lone parents, rely on grandparents for some or all of their childcare, for entirely understandable reasons.[5] It's immensely comforting to know your child is with someone you trust so implicitly, while Granny or Grandpa can be all that makes viable a job where wages are low or hours unsociable. And even the scattered nature of modern British family life doesn't seem to have cut the apron strings. I've known friends' parents commute to London weekly from Kent, Surrey, even Yorkshire for a day or two a week. During the manic years, my own career would never have survived without my mother's invaluable help from time to time. But I do wonder about the loneliness of the long-distance granny, pushing children on a swing so far from home, surrounded by strangers – and about quite how fair it is on grandparents who have already raised their own children to take on the full-time care of a whole new generation.

It is sorely tempting to wonder why our rather private, squeamish British families can't be more like the sprawling extended clans of romantic Mediterranean legend; after all, working women do seem to benefit from close-knit extended families. In her recent landmark study of Indian and Chinese working women,[6] the economist Sylvia Ann Hewlett found they expressed greater levels of ambition for top jobs than American graduates and seemed able to work long hours with less guilt than Western mothers because they weren't constantly worried about home. For the minority of wealthy and highly educated Indian women who enter elite professions, domestic work isn't really an issue: grandmothers take care of children and there are servants to deal with chores. As Chandra Kochhar, a mother of two who runs one of India's biggest banks (two out of three of which are run by women), puts it, 'We have a whole social network that enables women to manage a family. There is comfort in knowing you have a large joint family and household staff available.'[7]

Similarly in China, it's common for elderly people to live with their children and help out, and having older relatives living with them seems to make Chinese women more likely to work.[8] In the Philippines, which has the highest percentage of women in senior management positions in the world,[9] women benefit not just from cheap childcare and strong extended families but from a matriarchal society where men are used to women wielding power at home.

Yet these success stories are fragile, built on cheap labour and an extended family model which is already evolving, with young urban Indian parents increasingly experimenting with Western-style daycare. Last year the percentage of Indian women in work fell sharply, amid speculation in the Indian press that a non-working wife is now a status symbol for middle-class families – a sign that her husband is doing well enough to support them all. And Asian women do ultimately pay a price for grandparents' help: the majority of Indian and Chinese mothers in Hewlett's study admitted suffering from 'filial guilt', or a feeling that they should do more for their elders, which left them vulnerable to falling out of work as their parents aged. In Asia, the evidence suggests that grandparents are not a magic bullet.

Closer to home, we tell ourselves it's mutually beneficial. How nice for Mum to see so much of the grandchildren! But it's sometimes uncomfortably close to one-way traffic. Friends who rely heavily on grandparents whisper of guilt and obligation, being forced to bite their tongues over differences on sweets or television. As for the Mediterranean extended family, in Spain one union recently urged grandparents to go on strike under the slogans 'Learn to say no' and 'Don't feel guilty': its aim was to expose the lack of state-funded daycare and of flexible jobs which make Spanish families depend so much on grandparents in the first place. The time squeeze experienced by parents is being pushed upward through families, squeezing their parents instead, with sometimes bittersweet consequences for their own lives.

Many grandparents very much want to spend time with their grandchildren, of course, but they face new and competing claims on their time and energy. Over half of British grandparents are still at work themselves,[10] a number that will increase as pensions dwindle and the state retirement age rises. And, perhaps surprisingly, one recent survey of grandparents found that around twice as many of them looked after their own elderly parents as looked after their grandchildren.[11] This last is a classic indicator of the so-called 'beanpole families' created by increased life expectancy: long and stretched, they have fewer children than in times past but perhaps four generations of adults alive at the same time. The middle generations are torn in several directions at once, with some older people juggling work, ageing relatives and the grandchildren's school run at an age when they expected to find themselves pottering peacefully round the garden.

There is a whole different book to be written about the emerging battle over care, and I simply can't do justice to it here. Suffice it to say that as couples grow older, the 'wife time' carved out for home and children may well have to stretch to cover the care of elderly parents too; and that while grandparents do have a role to play in family life, it's both risky and unfair to expect them to fill the whole of the 'wife deficit' left by changing working patterns. We would do better to rethink the way families' time is deployed across the generations as well as across the sexes.

What might that look like in real life? Take a woman who first becomes a grandmother at 58. She no longer wants to work flat out, because she is looking forward to being a doting granny – but she can't quite afford to stop working either, because she needs to save more for retirement, and anyway she quite likes her job. So she negotiates with her boss to cut down to a three-day week. Now she spends Mondays with her grandson, and on Tuesdays she visits her own 90-year-old mother to do her shopping and go through her post and do all the other things that help her lead an independent life at home.

Meanwhile, her son has negotiated compressed hours, taking Fridays off. Her daughter-in-law, who might once have ended up a full-time mother because she couldn't face putting the baby in nursery all week, now works from home and takes Thursdays off. Between them all, the little boy is only in his expensive nursery two days a week: and his parents, no longer floundering in domestic chaos, can nip in to check on the great-grandmother on their days off.

All three of the adults in this family could, of course, in theory work flat out instead and pay professionals to care for the children and Great-Granny: but the emotional life of this family would be very different, and guilt might drive at least one of them to stop. Spreading the load in this way means they work eleven days between them – so they pay eleven days' worth of taxes, salt away eleven days' worth of pension contributions and spend what's left of eleven days' money in the wider economy – rather than the ten they might work between them if one adult gave up completely and the others worked full-time.

But to achieve this kind of solution, grandparents would need something stronger than their current patchy and contradictory rights over working time. As things stand, this grandmother can formally ask her boss for a day off a week to look after her own elderly mother, because the law gives rights to carers to request flexible working – but the same is not true of her day off to look after her grandchildren, because the law gives no such rights to grandparents. It's wrong for the state to value one kind of family care and not the other, especially since in real life they are often intimately interconnected, and grandparents should urgently be given the same rights as parents to vary their hours for childcare.

Not all families live near enough (or get on well enough) to make this kind of arrangement realistic. One of my great regrets about the way my family life is organised now is that I don't live nearer my parents. But the particularly galling thing is that I don't live nearer my sister, since, as Jane Austen once wrote to her niece, 'I have always maintained the importance of aunts.'

Shortly after my son was born, I was having lunch with three old friends when it struck me that all of the mobile phones on the table carried baby pictures as their screensavers. Yet I was, then, the only mother: the others were all fond aunts. One, who ran her own business, regularly bailed out a brother and sister-in-law both working long hours while raising two small children. Another didn't want children of her own, but doted on her niece. Suddenly I was reminded of how I felt when my first niece was born years before: that the intensity of the relationship with your sibling's children is oddly underestimated.

The fact that one in five women don't have children by the age of 45^{12} – some by choice, some sadly not – means a new breed of aunt or uncle with energy to invest in the extended family is emerging. Aunts and uncles are a unique blend of spare parent and friend, at one vital remove from the battlefield. They're not the ones nagging a child daily about picking up toys or finishing their homework, so what they say may occasionally actually sink in. If they have no children of their own to nag, they may also have both more energy and more empathy for a niece or nephew's point of view. And where two siblings both have children, the mutual ties of aunt and unclehood acquire even deeper meaning. Siblings who live nearby and both work flexibly can be perfect candidates for granting each other 'wife time'. I rather envy the idyllic-sounding set-up described by fashion designer Luella Bartley, who lives with her photographer partner and three children in a north Cornish farmhouse near the sea.

Her sister lives next door, with her partner and two children. Bartley, who until her eponymous label closed in 2009 was shuttling constantly between London and Cornwall, has said she set things up deliberately 'so the kids would have extended family. It's a bit of communal living.'[13]

It's an interesting choice of phrase. Full-blown communal living is still seen in Britain as primarily for students and squatters, yet some degree of more communitarian living with close friends or relatives when children are young can be surprisingly appealing. Reading the Liberal Democrat peeress Shirley Williams's biography recently, I was struck by her description of how she and her husband lived for seventeen years with friends, the literary agent Hilary Rubinstein and his wife. Her only daughter Rebecca had all the benefits of a bigger family life with the Rubinsteins' four children; both sets of parents pitched in domestically, leaving Williams free to spend her nights at the House of Commons. She wondered why more parents didn't try it. Closing the book, I wondered too – although perhaps it's only for friends who know each other as well as family. (Some of the same benefits might be gained from living in one of the Danish-style cohousing projects now springing up around the UK. Families live in separate houses but have access to a 'communal house' with shared facilities such as laundry, spare bedrooms for guests, and a dining hall in which they can eat together.)

For more conventional families, however, swapping 'wife time' between siblings can involve a basic fairness and reciprocity which doesn't exist with even the most stoical grandparent: you each get the same thing out of the deal, after all, and siblings are perhaps more likely to have similar ideas about discipline or routines, and similar energy levels.

'The benefits you get with family, you can't replace: the family upbringing and the fact that I call them interchangeable babies, my sister's and mine,' says Liz, whose sister lives only minutes away and has long traded childcare favours with her. 'Her children still call me "Mummy K" [her surname] or "Auntie K". I don't know how I would have coped if I had been giving them to somebody else to look after full time.' And above all, siblings can be a lifeline for those without a partner to offer 'wife time': single parents. Shift work is nearly impossible without someone at home to cover evenings and weekends, when formal childcare is vanishingly rare, and school holidays or everyday childhood illnesses are far harder to manage on your own.

Lee, who unexpectedly became the sole carer of his daughter when she was three months old, has a 'fantastically supportive sister without whom I would have gone absolutely mental'. Recent internal research for the Department for Work and Pensions estimates that 15 per cent of lone parents rely on their sisters for short term childcare and 5 per cent on their brothers, which when put together is more than could rely on the absent father. Among the examples found were two sisters who were both single mothers of only children, living and raising their children together while a third sister helped them out.

But for lone parents who can manage to keep some kind of civil relationship going with their ex-partner, divorce doesn't have to be the end of the joint parenting story. Nicola and Mike's separation, when their daughter was nearly two, was not amicable. 'We were both really mad at each other, and there is still resentment: we are not friends, we are a marriage that ended for good reasons,' she says. Yet they emerged from the wreckage with a rather fairer domestic deal than they managed during their marriage. They agreed Mike would have his daughter every other weekend and sometimes overnight in the week; as a result, Nicola finally got the sleep she craved. They are flexible about helping each other out in a crisis, and Nicola feels the split has left her better able to cope with her job as a social worker: 'My mobile was going off a hundred times a day, I'd never stop: a high proportion of my caseload were constantly in crisis. Without the extra time I got from us being separated, I don't know what would have happened to me.'

Nicola is now trying to set up a new business of her own, working from home around her daughter's school hours, but she is determined her ex-husband should remain part of this somewhat unorthodox family. 'We spend time around each other even though we drive each other mad, because I couldn't be Lily's mum without him there,' she says simply. 'I couldn't work, I couldn't get the new business off the ground. And she needs her daddy as much as she needs me.

'When your kids are ill, when they're babies and you have those awful nights – nobody tells you that you go crazy. You need somebody who you can ring just to say "she did this today" and know he'll get excited. We still operate as a family because we kind of are a family still.'

It helps that they're both unusually highly motivated to protect their daughter. Mike had had a previous bitter split, which affected his children from that marriage, while Nicola grew up in care and is fiercely determined to preserve a family life she didn't have for Lily. It may also help that they aren't formally divorced, so there was no acrimonious battle over assets. Although Nicola thinks she might have won a better financial deal by fighting her ex-husband in court, she seems resigned to letting that go in return for co-parenting and protecting her ability to earn. They still take major life decisions with each other in mind: 'We are her parents and we still consider our fortunes in terms of each other.' In coming chapters, we'll look at what it would take for more divorcing couples to carry on providing some of each other's 'wife time' even after the decree nisi.

So far, we have looked at ways to reduce the pressure on family life by drawing more adults into the care of children. But there is one last, more controversial way for working parents to ease the strain, and it's not to expand your family but to shrink it.

Two years ago, the Shanghai-based Hurun Report compiled a striking list of the world's richest self-made women which turned the conventional picture of female multimillionaires on its head: over half the women on the list were Chinese. While most of the wealthiest women in the West are heiresses to other people's money, Chinese women are making billions for themselves, and doing it surprisingly young. Several of the Hurun list were in their forties, precisely the time when many Western women drop out of contention. Their secret? The list's compiler Rupert Hoogewerf suggested that China's infamous one-child policy 'makes a huge difference' to the energy female entrepreneurs have to spare.[14] Mothers of only children may just have a competitive advantage.

A handful of female billionaires does not excuse the horrific cruelty of a Chinese family planning policy that has resulted in so much misery, forced abortion and involuntary sterilisation, of course. Draconian attempts to thwart parenthood are no platform on which to build the 'liberation' of working mothers. Yet ironically, a family structure imposed by force in China is spreading voluntarily – or more precisely, without need of legislation – in the West too.

Chinese birth rates are actually rising, as Beijing discreetly relaxes its iron grip on fertility; it's in countries where life for working parents is tough and the guilt pervasive, or where good childcare and flexible work aren't widespread, that young couples are hesitating and fertility is falling. Astonishingly, China's projected birth rate for 2010–15 was higher than that of Germany, Poland and even bambino-friendly Italy.[15] And although fertility has now picked up in Britain, there is an emerging trend towards the micro-family: in 1972, just 18 per cent of children were only children, but by 2007 it was 26 per cent. Our families are shrinking.

The sociologist Catherine Hakim has suggested bigger families are casualties of corporate life, noting that many successful British women are either childless or have what she calls 'nominal families' of one.[16] It's a fantastically offensive term, the 'nominal' parent, with its implication that only children don't really count – a kind of convenient family-lite, for those too selfish to have a proper one. But it's harder to dismiss the idea that family size is linked to success, and vice versa. After all, the difference between one child and two, a short and a long career break, can be the difference between a sustainable career and a wrecked one: parents of 'onlies' have more time, money and energy to spare. Is being 'done at one' a tactic adopted consciously or unconsciously, to create more time in overstretched lives?

When Andrew G. Marshall, therapist and author of the book on parental marriage *I love you but I'm not in love with you*, conducted a nationwide study on family size in 2010 he found that nearly a third of mothers still wanted another child; the depths of sadness exposed, says Marshall, 'completely knocked me away'.[17] Half of them blamed finances for the fact that they hadn't had more children, suggesting big families are now regarded as an unaffordable luxury. But like the myth that stay-at-home motherhood is only for the rich, it doesn't really hold water.

For parents already struggling to pay the mortgage, the prospect of doubling the nursery fees can indeed be prohibitive. But the desire to make babies seems to have surprisingly little to do with financial reality. Pakistani and Bangladeshi families are twice as likely as white British families to say they want more than two children,[18] but statistically far more likely to be poor; and while the percentage of couples with three or more children has halved since 1971,[19] the percentage of single mothers with big families has tripled. Whatever else they may be, single parents are rarely stinking rich.

Marshall thinks the financial argument is really about fearing you couldn't provide such a high standard of living for another child: 'We don't think "can we feed another one?" It's more like "oh, they're going to need their own bedroom". In the past children sharing bedrooms was nothing – they probably would have been sharing beds.' But to me that doesn't quite explain why, as the population expert Warren S. Thompson put it to the American magazine *Science Newsletter*, 'You hear people say "we cannot afford more children", but it is not the very poor who feel that way: it is the relatively well-to-do.'

He was writing back in 1939, amid a panic about couples having too few children that would lead five years later in Britain to the creation of a Royal Commission on Population. It duly concluded that smaller families had been an economic advantage ever since Western economies shifted from the farm (where children could help with the harvest) to the factory. The invention of reliable birth control and women's growing interest in a life beyond motherhood had just intensified the trend. The birth rate first began falling around 1870, as jobs opened up for women in mills, shops and offices – which would suggest that working patterns do influence family size, and if the Hurun rich list is right, perhaps vice versa.

The modern shrinking family is surely at least partly to do with fear of the damage another child would do to a career already knocked sideways by the last baby, or about fearing that childcare would price the mother out of work (mothers of three are significantly less likely to work than mothers of two).[20] And for those women who now find themselves sole earners, things are even more complicated. Cathy, a teacher whose husband is at home full-time with their two children, is not pushing for the third child she might otherwise have liked because to compensate for the expense of another maternity leave she would have to chase a promotion she doesn't want: 'I love teaching, and I don't want to have to climb higher.' All that lies above her are desk-bound jobs offering less and less time at the chalkface.

Later motherhood, which may mean mothers managing to conceive one child but running out of time to have another, is almost certainly a big factor – but even that can't be entirely disentangled from work. The gap between what a woman could earn over her lifetime if she didn't have children, and the amount she'll earn as a mother – eroded by career breaks, going part-time, discrimination or trading down in seniority in order to get flexibility – is known as the 'motherhood penalty'. A mid-skilled woman who has her first child at 24 loses twice as much over a lifetime as a woman who first gives birth at 30.[21] Young women may not have these figures at their fingertips, but every time they see women slightly higher up the ladder sliding back down past them after having children, they grasp the general idea. The economic risks of having children young are every bit as real to them as the much more widely publicised biological risks of having children late.

There's probably never a 'right' time to have children, but for what it's worth, here are a few hard facts: a woman's chances of failing to get pregnant within a year of trying naturally are six times higher at 35 than at 25. But since infertility is quite rare in young women, that still means 70 per cent of women who start trying at 35 will get pregnant naturally within the year.[22] Even by 40, a surprising four in ten women will conceive naturally in a year of trying, although they face a significantly greater risk of miscarriage. In other words, later motherhood is a gamble but not an impossible one: and early motherhood is a gamble too, since couples marrying young are more likely to divorce. Late motherhood is, for many women, arguably a practical response to circumstances not of their choosing.

The shrinking family has not been without pain, as I would be the first to acknowledge. On paper, I am the classic mother who ran out of time myself: pregnant easily at 35, a rather complacent 37 before I seriously considered having another one, and a chastened 39 by the time we entered the infertility clinic. The young registrar was mechanically upbeat about the prospects for IVF, growing testy only when I started to question his casual optimism.

I'm still not entirely sure why I hesitated. Like most women my age, I have seen enough friends experience IVF to know it can be both risky and gruelling and that the odds are always heavily weighted towards failure. And we had one beautiful, clever little boy: was that not enough? Why provoke the gods? I wavered for all these reasons; but also, if I am honest, because while I wanted a second child, I wasn't consumed by that desire to the exception of all else. I could see some advantages to life with one child, who was growing more independent every day, over being sucked back into the lovely but all-consuming vortex of early motherhood: I could see my life widening out again, and him enjoying the luxury of all our time and attention. It isn't what I would have chosen. But the elusiveness of another baby created a fork in the road, a decision to be made between my maternal and other selves. As Andrew Marshall puts it, 'It becomes harder to have another child once you are actually back at work and become re-established.' As I write, I am a parent of one not by choice but not entirely by accident either. After all, I deliberately waited to tick all the professional boxes I wanted to tick before starting a family, having watched other new mothers vanish from Fleet Street. I made decisions knowing they might have consequences, although hoping they wouldn't. And I doubt I'm alone.

It's not easy for parents to admit openly that they don't want more children or are even ambiguous about it, although 14 per cent of the parents of only children in Marshall's survey said they had always actively wanted one. As the social statistician Julie Jefferies puts it, 'Parents of only children . . . risk being considered selfish for not providing their child with a sibling to interact with and being thought of as only marginally committed to parenthood.'[23] But her analysis of mothers of one child finds an intriguing difference depending on the mother's age: those under 34 were more likely definitely to want another baby, but a majority of older mothers were either keen to stop there, or undecided.[24] Do some women unconsciously leave motherhood late precisely because they were not earth mother types in the first place?

Only children are not the answer to a working parent's dilemma. But they're not invariably tragic either, as parents of larger broods should remember before saying 'Just the one?' with that ghastly mix of curiosity and head-cocked sympathy. The view that only children will be either overbearing 'little emperors' or sad, friendless waifs is now crumbling under the weight of evidence.

It's not surprising that only children regularly score higher on tests of intelligence and self-esteem, since they soak up their parents' undivided attention. But as long ago as 1987, a landmark review of the evidence by the psychologist Toni Falbo (an only child, and parent of one) found that only children scored similarly to children with siblings on tests for personality traits including generosity, co-operativeness and how independent and self-reliant they were.[25] Translation: they're neither appallingly selfish, nor clingy.

As for the 'lonely only', a study of over 13,000 American teenagers led by sociologist Donna Bobbitt-Zeher in 2010 found they had as many friends as those with siblings.[26] Her co-researcher had previously found that only children's social skills were slightly worse in kindergarten, but they seem to catch up by around the age of 10 – and with most toddlers now routinely in preschool, they may get more early practice at making friends. As studies like this one start to dispel the myths and stigma that surround only children, it's possible more parents will choose to be 'done at one'; if nothing else, since there is a powerful drive to recreate the family we grew up in, the mere fact of more children growing up without siblings may mean more becoming parents of 'onlies' in turn, with potentially interesting consequences for their working lives.

The focus in this chapter on solving the time squeeze within families may seem naïve to some, and certainly shouldn't be seen as a homespun alternative to action by employers and government. Families don't pay taxes in order to watch the state wriggle out of its rightful responsibilities. But it is important to separate out what individuals can do by themselves from what can only be done by governments – and not just because the latter tend to move far more slowly, grudgingly and nervously. Any career is vulnerable unless it's built on solid ground, namely a fair deal within the home and a broad base of support from family and friends beyond it. Only when this foundation is in place can parents really move on to think about the nature of work itself.

7

THE GLASS ELEVATOR

Back in the days when Kate Grussing worked for a big City bank, her one 'great indulgence' to herself was doing the school run on a Friday morning. As a team leader in a senior management role, the mother of four was resigned to not being able to work part-time, something that worried her for more than personal reasons. 'I realised that if a senior woman couldn't be part-time, God help the junior women. So I looked at what the firm could do to promote part-time work.' To her surprise, what she found was that colleagues working in her bank's American sister operation were five times as likely to be working part-time. 'Same culture, same clients, same work demands. And the firms have the same policies,' as Grussing puts it. Yet these plum part-time jobs were possible in America, but not across the Atlantic.

It was a wake-up call for Grussing in the art of the possible and so eight years ago she left the City, planning to start up a specialist recruitment practice dealing in high-end part-time corporate jobs with good pay and prospects. The conventional agencies she approached with her idea were, she recalls, baffled by it; but all those Friday mornings at the school gates, mingling with other mothers who had fallen out of traditional corporate life, had convinced her there was a market. And so a defiant Grussing set up her own specialist firm of headhunters, Sapphire Partners, instead.

Thanks in part to enlightened recruiters like Grussing, it's no longer impossible to find challenging, stimulating jobs with good pay and prospects that still allow time for a family. But there aren't enough of them, even though, as the experience of Grussing's former American colleagues suggests, it can be easier than companies think to create these kinds of positions. In coming chapters, we'll look at what both employers and governments can do to create a genuine market in flexible jobs that also works to their advantage.

But first, I want to look at what parents can do to help themselves – for if you are already at the stage of weeping in the office loo every morning, you need to deal with the world as it is rather than as it should be. What can men and women do to negotiate the hours they want more effectively, to deal with the inevitable resistance to using their working time differently, and even to plan their careers more intelligently from the outset?

In the natural world, where energy meets resistance it tends to abandon the straight line. Boats tack against the wind, roads carve uphill in a series of hairpin bends, and even lightning zigzags to the ground against the sullen weight of the air. The beauty of zigzagging is that it's good for getting round obstacles: and this makes the Z shape a very useful way of thinking about the ideal working parent's career.

What many parents want is to be able to alternate periods of shooting up the ladder with sideways moves when the clash between work and life becomes too much – but without sacrificing the potential of another rise in future. A working life that followed this pattern would look less like a straight line and more like an interlinked chain of Zs. It would start with a horizontal line, representing the time spent in school and university preparing for work, and after graduation would come the first upward stroke of the 'Z'. With neither children nor elderly parents to look after yet, most of us in our twenties have the stamina and the energy to clock up long hours and compete ferociously, making this a turbo-boosted phase of working life during which we can first get established and then get promoted.

The first sidestep would come some time after 30, the average age at which women have their first babies – and couples start wanting half a wife. These are the classic years of parents seeking to take relatively large chunks of time out with preschool children, of parental leave and part-time working, and they form the second horizontal line at the top of the imaginary 'Z'. It may be a time of treading water rather than making progress, but if it's carefully planned, it can be followed by another upward stroke a few years later when the children are at school and the fog of exhaustion clears.

By now, parents aren't looking to be at home all day, but often still need some give around the edges: working from home at times, working flexitime with an earlier start or finish, or being self-employed start to appeal.

Some parents will then want to take a second short sidestep again later, either to spend more time looking after elderly parents or during the highly pressurised GCSE and A-level years. Children's need for their parents becomes less frequent but sometimes more urgent now, and more personal. Pretty much any loving adult can change a nappy, but persuading a rebellious teenager back on to the rails takes someone they know very well.

On the other side of 50, as children head off to work and college, lies a hugely underestimated potential for another upward stroke of the Z: for women in particular, the last two decades of work can bring a sudden, intoxicating third wind. When Harriet

Harman ran for the deputy leadership of the Labour Party at the age of 57, she explained that since her children had grown up 'I have a sense of how much more I can do.' Parents are now free to throw themselves into work with renewed energy.

The historian Pat Thane points to a long tradition of women being liberated by the end of childbearing: as far back as medieval Europe, women gained more independence and occasionally even public roles after the menopause – perhaps as midwives, or adjudicators in community conflicts, building on the acknowledged skills of mothering.[1] Children growing up spelled the end of a life led largely behind closed doors. As the writer Joanna Moorhead put it last year, 'No longer do I feel that being a mother is my foremost occupation. Somewhere inside – and sometimes quite angrily – I have started to think that not only do I matter too, but that time I have left to matter is considerably reduced.'[2] It's the ticking of a very different but no less urgent biological clock. Despite the youthful image of entrepreneurship, a quarter of new businesses in Britain are now started by the over-fifties, either cashing in on a lifetime's experience and contacts for a little more freedom or frustrated by what's on offer in the conventional job market.[3]

It's not childbearing, but ageism that holds back the older zigzagger: the recession hasn't been kind to older workers. But the underlying trend since the early 1990s has nonetheless been for steadily rising employment rates for the over-fifties, and it's driven by women. The numbers of older women working leapt by 14 per cent between 1996 and 2008, against just 4 per cent for older men.[4] My guess is, that isn't just about changes like the outlawing of age discrimination at work; it's about changes in older women themselves.

The current generation of over-fifties are children of the 1960s: they're more likely than their mothers were to have degrees, more likely to have had careers before children (not just a job until they married) and to have worked afterwards, although often part-time. They're not 'empty nesters', forlorn housewives scrabbling for something to do now their children are grown and gone, but women with solid CVs. Many are walking adverts for the benefits of keeping up 'half a life': some purposeful activity outside the home, even if it's just for a few hours a week.

So beyond this last potential sprint upwards lies another sideways step, or the top of the last Z: a gradual fade out of work, perhaps via part-time or consultancy roles, into retirement. Even during the recession, a third of the new jobs created in 2010 actually went to people above state pension age, according to the Office of National Statistics; experienced and reliable, but no longer keen to work long hours, they perfectly matched the largely part-time jobs being created.

Mapping work across the life cycle like this reveals a need to change direction and reinvent careers more often than many of us perhaps expect. But when working life spans half a century, as later retirement suggests it will for my generation, does anybody really want to spend it all doing the same thing? Or would we be better served by two or three careers, linked by a common thread, spread over different phases of our lives?

In fifty years of working life, there should be no shame in having periods when you are frankly coasting for a bit (if working while being woken three times a night by a baby can ever be described as coasting), easing the strain on the 'concertina years' of intense pressure both at work and at home. 'We are moving slightly closer to the American idea that there is nothing weird about working at 72 and I think that potentially has great opportunities for women,' says headhunter Deborah Loudon. 'If that becomes more of a norm people can be quite a bit more relaxed.'

And over such a long working lifespan, there would be even less shame in having periods when you are not necessarily moving up, but still absorbed in something interesting. But a successful zigzag career requires the ability to make strategic rather than tactical moves, continuing to tell a logical story rather than just clutching in desperation at any old job with shorter hours.

That might mean starting with a core qualification, such as law or accountancy, and riffing off it in different ways over the years: a trained lawyer might start out working very long hours for good money in a law firm, but jump to being an in-house lawyer for a big company after having children (better hours, although perhaps more repetitive work); or to a charity (better hours, more meaningful work, but worse money) or into lecturing, or into a non-executive directorship or public appointment where legal skills are sought after. It might mean retraining or studying in midlife, keeping a sideline going alongside a job, being ready to switch roles or companies or sectors. But essentially it means seeing your skills, experiences, reputation and contacts as a pivot: a base on which you can quickly swivel to face in another direction, if you need to.

If all this sounds too good to be true, it needn't be: some working parents are beginning to build careers that look very much like this, even within conventional corporate life. But there are very good reasons why many of the parents I interviewed had chosen to do it by working for themselves. Self-employment classically rises in a recession, when there aren't enough conventional jobs to go round, but it's a life raft for those failed or frustrated by conventional work even in good times, which might be why female-only start-ups increased by 9 per cent in the last year of the boom.[5] And it's one of the few ways men feel comfortable about leaving the conventional career track.

*

For some reason while women starting their own businesses are patronisingly branded 'mumpreneurs' and portrayed as having done it to fit round their children, men who start businesses are portrayed as risk-taking buccaneers. The reality for many women entrepreneurs, particularly if the venture takes off, clearly defies the image: Cath Kidston's eponymous business may be built on cosy domesticity, but she rather endearingly told one interviewer that she was so absorbed in work that her husband was 'lucky if he gets a takeaway, quite honestly'.[6] So I often wonder how many male escapees from corporate life might be hiding family-friendly hours behind the macho, workaholic image of the 'manpreneur'. A useful maxim for the self-employed is, 'Never apologise, never explain.' Although I nearly always work the same three days a week, if a new client calls on a non-working day I'll often just say I'm busy with another project. Only I need know the 'project' is a play-date. So long as I deliver, it is nobody's business but mine how I spend my time: and working like this is a great way for men to rake back one or two days by stealth.

Dan, a father of two daughters aged 10 and 14, runs his own marketing business mostly from home, and a successful blog. He originally gave up his full-time job because it became clear he and his wife were being pulled in too many directions at once by their careers. 'I quit working full-time because with the amount that goes on in our lives, it would have been extremely difficult to sustain that with two of us working long hours,' he says. 'It's kind of like, how much money do you need?' His wife now works four days a week in the entertainment industry, while he estimates that work takes up about two-thirds of his week. The rest revolves around school runs, household tasks and the girls: 'I'm the primary runner around. I do the play-dates and sleepovers. Friendships – that's difficult because I end up making terrible mistakes, my advice on those things is inevitably wrong. I'm now just a shoulder to cry on.' Although Dan says his wife is very good at switching off from work the minute she comes through the door, because his work is flexible and from home, he's the one the girls can most easily interrupt.

Working from home, after all, often isn't just about avoiding the commute. Once you are no longer tied to the office, you may well find yourself liberated from keeping office hours as well. So long as the work is done by the end of the day, it often doesn't matter if you got up early to do it and then knocked off mid-afternoon for the school run: after all, nobody's watching over your shoulder. My own life now feels less like working part-time and more like working *smarter*, arranging time the way *I* want it. So while on average I work about three days a week, I don't keep fixed hours. I may end up doing almost five days' work in three, working well into the night, or I may do far less.

The price paid for this more weightless life, of course, is work seeping into the evenings. I didn't want to become that horrible cliché, the woman so busy writing about motherhood that she forgets to do any actual mothering: so I have traded many afternoons messing around in the garden for long evenings' penance on the computer. While in theory I have written this book, built up a freelance journalism career and sat on two policy-making commissions all while working the three days a week for which I have childcare, the truth is that I often took on too much and tackled the overspill at night. It's tough on spouses and can be exhausting, but occasionally working by night so you can parent by day makes sense: while singletons are nocturnal animals, frankly parents of small children often don't do a whole lot with their evenings. Self-employment is a natural fit for a particular breed of driven parent who may want not so much to halve their hours as to rearrange them – and also, perhaps, for anyone who feels stuck in a rut. While staying on part-time at my old newspaper would almost certainly have meant going backwards, leaving has opened up a world of new possibilities. It was the only way I could see to shrink my hours but expand my professional horizons, to keep moving forwards and trying new things.

Perhaps the best thing about freelancing, however, is the joy of being free to do what you love, unplugged. Stripping away the meetings and memos can make the work itself sing, which is perhaps one reason why a third of interim managers surveyed by the interim agency Russam GMS said they found the work more interesting than a conventional management career. They don't stay long enough to be drawn into office politics or bogged down in the daily grind, so they can spend their time problem-solving. Personally, I never knew how much I enjoyed writing until I was free to just do it.

And the more I do it, the more secure self-employment feels. Having a range of clients spreads the risk of any one relationship turning sour: it allows you to diversify your way out of trouble in ways you might never have thought of inside a company, and to use your time with a satisfyingly selfish efficiency. 'One of the things I've realised is that I get certain things done more quickly than somebody else would,' says Jane, of her new career as a consultant. 'That benefit I think should be my benefit: if I get the work done quicker I can then go and do something else. I wouldn't go back to a culture where I have to sit in the office just because everyone else is.' Having turned herself into a limited company, she estimates that tax perks mean she is also no worse off than when working full-time.

Some parents I interviewed used the zigzag out of paid work to reinvent themselves completely. Colette set herself up as a freelance marketing consultant after leaving a similar in-house job, but quickly got frustrated by not seeing projects through. When a former client let slip she was giving up her online business selling children's travel products, Colette saw the potential in the business and rather impulsively bought it. 'The decision was made very quickly, and then over the Christmas holiday we drove up and picked up her remaining stock in a dodgy van at a motorway service station, with my husband shaking his head and saying "What are we doing?"' she recalls. 'And that's how it started.'

Web-based businesses appeal to working parents because they can be nurtured outside office hours. Colette processes new orders in the evenings, wrapping deliveries overnight and taking them to the post office during the day accompanied by her daughter. Her son is in primary school now and her daughter at nursery two mornings a week, but beyond that she has no childcare and works around them. Her working from home has enabled the family to swap city life for rural Dorset. Her husband, a town planner, now works locally with a short commute by bike along the beach, which means he can also now pitch in with the children in the evenings.

The lowest-risk route to self-employment is usually freelancing using a proven skill, with few start-up costs beyond clearing space on the dining room table. Evolution rather than revolution is often a safer bet, particularly if you suspect you may one day want to return to the beaten track. 'It's quite important to see a hook to what you did before rather than doing something totally different: what people look at when they're hiring is a coherent narrative,' says Deborah Loudon. It also gives you time and space to discreetly change your mind. In her 2003 book *Working Identity*, the academic Herminia Ibarra rather sensibly advocates allowing three to five years for a major career change and granting yourself 'a transition period in which it is okay to oscillate between holding on and letting go' of the old professional self, rather than expecting everything to happen overnight.

Jess is now well past this three-year tidemark, and moving from the sideways phase of the zigzag into a second leap up the ladder. She was the deputy editor of a magazine when she got pregnant, but gave up work to be a full-time mother; her own mother had walked out on her when she was a baby, and she admits she was subconsciously trying to be the perfect mother she never had. With hindsight she thinks her husband, who wasn't particularly attached to his career in the media, might have been willing to be the primary carer, but at the time it barely occurred to her: 'I had this earth mother thing because my father had brought me up. I had my father all the time and not my mother. I was trying to right what I perceived to be this wrong.'

After her son was born, Jess quickly realised she had made a mistake. Work had been a huge part of her identity, as had her pride in being able to support herself, and she suffered a serious bout of post-natal depression which made her aware of what she had lost. By the time her son was a year old, she had plucked up the courage to start over again by approaching a parenting magazine with some ideas.

Jess began by working way below her old seniority and salary, but as she puts it, 'It was work so I did it.' After her second baby, she bounced back even more confidently. Now the boys are aged six and three, her career is unmistakably on the upswing again, although she continues to work mainly from home and chooses her hours to suit her. 'I do things now that I never thought I would do before I had kids: there is absolutely no doubt that my career is in much better shape now. I do loads of broadcasting, I have got a literary agent, I am writing a book, I am now a columnist. There's absolutely no way I will ever work full-time ever again. I like the freedom of being freelance too much.'

Jess's story is a good example of how self-employment can mean a more relaxed and a far more interesting life: she's not so much dropped out of a good career as dropped into several new ones.

It has also led to a much more equal distribution of the 'wife work' in the family. She and her husband now share the childcare roughly 50/50, with the help of an au pair.

For those who don't quite have the professional nerve to strike off on their own, there is a halfway house emerging in some industries between self-employment and working for a company. The 'virtual company' model, where a firm might have only a few permanent staff co-ordinating a network of freelance consultants called in as and when jobs demand, has brought a new way of working into white-collar industries from management consultancy to PR. Each consultant commonly chooses whether or not they want to work on any given project: they might work largely from home, or choose to take on a project for a set time and then take time off. Virtual companies can offer the freedom of freelancing while still providing shelter beneath the umbrella of a bigger 'brand'. At their best, they let experienced professionals cash in on their reputations and work the hours they want.

The downside of 'cloud labour' – so-called because it's hovering just overhead, drawn down only when necessary – is of course exploitation: risks that used to be shouldered by employers, such as building a pension, are pushed unceremoniously back on to the employee. And while a slow few months in a conventional law firm are the company's problem, since they still have to pay your salary, a slow few months in a virtual company quickly become your problem. Parents would also do well to beware some of the 'microtasking' websites now springing up which match freelance IT workers, graphic designers or secretaries with work via a kind of auction process, where you name your own hourly price. They have an inbuilt tendency to bargain wages down, since it's tempting to get work by undercutting other site users. It's one thing wafting into the cloud if you are a £200,000 a year lawyer exploiting niche expertise, another for a low earner in a crowded market whose main selling point is being desperate enough to do it cheaper.

Financial risks aside, self-employment requires a much more active approach to a career: there are no annual pay rises or automatic promotions, and nobody to steer your career except you, which means the self-employed must be capable of constant reinvention. You must save harder to build up the same pension as those who benefit from employers' contributions, and there is always the nagging fear that work will dry up, making it hard to turn anything down. Mortgages are tough to obtain and maternity allowance for the self-employed is miserly, so it can make sense to stay on the payroll if possible until the family is complete.

For all these reasons, leaving formal employment isn't for everyone and it certainly isn't a decision to be taken lightly. It makes sense to try and negotiate a sabbatical, or if your children are under five to try and use your right to up to four weeks a year of unpaid parental leave, before quitting outright. Spending a few weeks thinking soberly about whether you want to be your own boss, or merely hate your current boss, can be worth double the lost pay. There is more than one way to trade the career you've built up in return for a life, but it takes careful planning.

'One of our problems was what do you do if you have probably had the best job in your life when you are 27?' says Tim, who like his wife Julia had unusually large amounts of responsibility when he was in his twenties. 'But it's what you build the rest of your career on afterwards. That was the time we worked incredibly long hours and all the rest of it. And in retrospect it was a good time to have done it.' One of the reasons Julia was able to wangle a four-day week was her strong negotiating position, because she has a relatively niche set of skills that the company badly needed. (It probably also helped that her new firm has a tradition of employees working from home on Fridays, so the fact that she

wanted Fridays off completely didn't seem so unusual.) Her new
job may not be as exciting as her early career, but on the plus
side both parents can spend time with their two small children
while creating a solid base from which their careers can take off
again.

With their youngest child coming up to school, Tim was already
considering upshifting again. Not long after we spoke, he took a
director-level job with an international company. But he still plans
to work a day from home: like Dan and his wife, who still work
a four-day week each although their youngest child is now 10,
he can't see the family returning to conventional working life in
a hurry. 'I don't think we will ever both be doing a standard nine
to five. We might both be doing big corporate jobs with more
flexible hours but I can't imagine while the kids are both still
quite young us doing what we used to do,' he says. 'If you can
avoid doing it, why would you want to?'

But being able to cash in your chips in this way – to trade off
the skills and reputation built up before children – means giving
much more thought to the chips you collect in the early stages
of a career. The single biggest difference young men and women
could make to their future prospects for flexible working is to
choose a career carefully in the first place.

Since one of the most common reasons men's formal requests
to work flexibly are rejected is that they work in inflexible places,
it's madness that we do not encourage young men to think even
broadly about how their choice of career (and company) will
shape their lives as fathers. Barely a year goes by without a girls'
school headmistress hitting the headlines for warning her charges
that they can't have it all – but who talks to teenage boys about
how family life and ambition fit together? Conventional careers
advice for both sexes focuses more on matching an individual to
a job than on planning a career that will evolve throughout the

life cycle, and that leaves a gaping hole, since at the age when most of us choose our careers children can be as distantly unimaginable as a foreign country. The nagging question is whether it's kinder to encourage a belief in those just starting out on working life that everything is possible, or to be more brutally honest about the trade-offs – and about the complex ways in which having children may affect their feelings about work.

What happens to ambition when we have children is for me best explained by one of the two founding laws of physics. The first law of thermodynamics states that energy can't be created or destroyed: it can be stored for a while, or change form, but it never dies. And I think that's roughly what happens to ambition in many parents.

In the early months it's often stored in parenting, and after that there can indeed be a powerful desire to channel it into something different. But ambition is rarely completely destroyed, and that's what bothers me most about the seductive idea that mothers 'naturally' lose interest in their careers. The choices women make about work can't be separated from the cultural and indeed practical context in which they make them – and the British context is still too often one in which successful women are unfairly labelled as pushy, unfeminine, and quasi-neglectful of their children. Why compete, if you'll be despised for winning?

That said, what really infuriates me about the lazy assumption that motherhood makes women less driven is a nagging suspicion that in my case it was true. I just didn't feel quite the same about my job after having a baby. I didn't lie awake at night kicking myself over the inevitable story that got away. But with hindsight I think what I lost wasn't ambition, but fear. Once my son was born, and with him the lifelong terror every parent has of anything ever happening to the children, it became instantly clear that there were worse things in life than missing out on an interview with Gordon Brown.

The irony is, I was probably a better political editor for it: bolder, less risk averse, less inclined to sweat the small stuff. But for the first time in years, I was also restless. Since work was now something I actively chose to do instead of being with my son, I expected more from it. But once I was no longer willing to work 60 hours a week, I simply couldn't see an interesting job on the paper that fitted the time I had to give.

Several of the parents I interviewed were clearly worried about the messages they were sending their daughters by surrendering high-profile careers, and conflicted about what to tell them as they grew up. 'Is it better that you are a role model, or that they have you at home?' wonders Polly, who has two daughters. 'I think it would have been better if my mum had had an insight into something beyond the kitchen. Will my daughters turn round and say "I can't believe you gave up"?' It's not just parents of girls who worry about that. I can still remember, shortly before I left my job, smuggling my then two-year-old son on to the floor of the Commons when the chamber was empty one night, and letting him clamber up on the green leather bench to bang on the prime minister's dispatch box. Looking back, I think I wanted to make my job come alive for him, to show him that mummies can and do belong somewhere other than home. These days I worry more about what to tell him, when he grows up, about where daddies belong.

With a bit of imagination, it should be possible to teach children to plan for a future family life without lowering their sights. While parents who want to take the long summer holidays off with their children might once have been encouraged into teaching, Kate Grussing suggests the better-paid profession of accountancy: work peaks at the end of the financial year and summers are slow, meaning some big firms will now consider versions of term-time working. Grussing herself worked for a time as a management consultant, which she also recommends for flexibility because it's project-based: project lengths can be adjusted to cope with shorter working weeks, and periods of intensive work interspersed with lighter months. 'A law firm is very "up or out" and doesn't have a lot of alternative career paths. A consultancy will have realised that there's lots of different career paths.'

The basic rule of thumb is that if a job can't ever be done freelance, from home or part-time, and doesn't involve a core professional skill (like a law qualification) which can be adapted to different settings, then anyone who wants to see anything of their future children should ask themselves seriously how much they want it. A career that can be done conventionally and intensively in your twenties, but in other ways later if necessary, is worth its weight in gold (or at least in salary not sacrificed).

And it can help, too, to think about precisely what we mean by a 'successful' career. One reason women don't reach the top in the same numbers as men, according to research on leadership carried out by the management consultancy McKinsey,[7] is that they tend to stick at a level where they feel they are making a difference. They recoil from the rather pointless power games they see played out higher up, without which of course it isn't possible to reach the top. But if those are the rules of the game, do we really have to play? Who says success means a big fat salary, bagging a corner office, wielding control over others – and not doing what you love or making things happen; not wielding control over your own life? 'There's an assumption in which to progress you have to do more at a senior level. We are arguing you can build your skills and move up on the skills ladder without having to take more hours,' says Emma Stewart, co-founder of Women like Us. 'Why should progress mean doing more work, longer hours?'

Unhappy but ambitious parents should ask themselves this: is it worth the pain of trying to batter headfirst through a glass ceiling, or would it make more sense to walk out and look for the lifts? The great benefit of a glass elevator is that it may stop at several different floors along the way, and sometimes go down before going up, but at least you enjoy the view.

Stewart's business partner Karen Mattison says many parents returning to work after children find they no longer want to play the corporate game in the same way. 'Returners who want a senior role are less interested in power and more interested in influence. We will hear "I want to make a difference if I am going to leave the kids, I want to do something that means something."' And working out where influence, rather than power, lies in any given profession can be a good way of snuffling out interesting flexible jobs.

Having power in the office is time-consuming: it usually means supervising other people, and therefore being available when they are. Often it means watching your back, matching the efforts (and hours) of others who want that power. But influence doesn't require managing people below you so much as being trusted by the people above you, and therefore able to steer and shape their decisions. Influence is about cashing in on the time you've already put into a career, being valued for your judgement and experience rather than your hours. Power is being a government minister, working 80 hours a week: influence is working four days a week for the think tank that generates the ideas politicians are too exhausted to think of for themselves. Power is running a team: influence is being brought in to advise on reorganising that team. While freelances are often perceived as being lower status than permanent staff, surprisingly often it's the other way round: pay an 'expert' for their services and you tend to take them seriously, because otherwise it reflects badly on your judgement in hiring them. As Olivia, who works as a freelance human resources consultant, puts it, 'People listen to you because they're paying you for the day – you don't have to work a political machine to get a meeting.' Influential careers often aren't as well paid as powerful ones, but the truth is there are remarkably few jobs that offer flexible hours, maximum salary and high status: and if you don't want to put in long hours, then chasing influence rather than power is a good way of maintaining status and seniority at least. You may not rise as high, but you might well have a more interesting life.

But what really makes the difference in creating a successful Z-shaped career is one thing a lot of working parents simply aren't very good at: the art of negotiation, both on the sideways leg of the Z (so that you can move into a job that's less demanding but still interesting) and on the upwards leg (so that you can move back into something more demanding when the time is right).

In their classic text *Women Don't Ask*, Linda Babcock and Sara Laschever set out in grim detail how women's poor negotiating skills drag down their earnings over a lifetime. Almost nine in ten female graduates in their study simply accepted the starting salary they were offered in their first job: but half the men tried to haggle it up, and a significant proportion succeeded. While the men realised that fighting about money was part of the game, the women tended to trust the company to play fair – even though logically, it was in their interest to pay as little as possible – and to worry that playing hardball would make them less likeable.

Speaking as a spectacularly hopeless negotiator of pay rises during my time on Fleet Street, it doesn't take a huge leap of imagination to wonder whether negotiation is the first weak link in both sexes' attempts to change their working patterns. New mothers enter talks over the return from maternity leave naïvely assuming the company will do the right thing and wholly unprepared for how hard they might have to fight; it doesn't help that they already feel beholden for having had time off. Men's preference for ducking out and working flexibly by stealth, meanwhile, suggests that they feel far less confident about negotiating over time than over money: asking for a rise goes with the grain of cultural assumptions about men as providers, but asking for more time does the opposite.

Employers have a moral and a legal responsibility to handle these conversations better, of course. But until that happy day, parents should know that negotiating is a knack that can be learned. Most research shows that women who act 'male' in pay discussions, demanding what's rightfully theirs, are marked down for being too pushy. But as any young lawyer learns in court, there is a skill to negotiating well: knowing when to push and when to give ground, how to win without the other person losing face, how to identify your own and the other side's weak points. It is astonishing, given what women in particular stand to lose from doing it badly, that negotiation isn't taught in sixth forms, universities or on subsidised training courses offered by unions. But after a year of collecting advice from people who negotiate rather better than I do, a handful of tips stand out.

It may prove helpful when trying to negotiate shorter hours, home working or any other flexible option to suggest a trial period – say three to six months – giving parents a chance to prove it can work (and discreetly job-hunt if it doesn't). Kate Grussing regularly places clients in senior part-time roles on a temporary basis, often a four-day week for a six-month period. 'Half of those turn into permanent options because the person has proved themselves, and the client gets it that they are getting 100 per cent of someone's brain if not their time,' she says. For senior roles, she thinks it can make a critical difference if you can commit to swapping days off occasionally or being available in a crisis. 'You can't say "sorry, I don't work Fridays, full stop" unless you want to do something lower skilled.'

Men in particular may also want to consider asking for reduced hours not through the formal 'right to request' but as part of a negotiation they're already familiar with and often good at: the annual pay round. Wages are likely to stay frozen or rise by less than inflation this year in industries hard hit by recession, leaving managers with empty pockets: time, rather than money, is often the only bribe left to offer people they want to keep. Having the conversation about working time in the context of a more traditional one about pay can help managers see it as part of the retention process, and arguably make men feel more comfortable about asking.

Grussing also advises men to be upfront in negotiations about why they want to do something different, since hedging will only arouse suspicions. 'Employers will always be interested to understand the whole person. If someone is a father of four children, or he's really active in running the local sports club, that helps a client understand and rationalise and accept that just because the person isn't here one day a week doesn't mean he's not contributing.'

The one golden rule all the recruitment experts I consulted agreed on was never to give up work completely, if humanly possible. While some parents do bounce back from long career breaks, it's an awful lot easier to talk your way out of work than to talk yourself back in. 'The longer you are away the harder it is to imagine yourself having skills and experience that the world out there wants,' says Karen Mattison. 'When you are in work, you can imagine reskilling or "If I wasn't doing this then I could do this . . ."' Working one day a week is a lot better than nothing, especially if you have qualifications that must be kept current (as in nursing) or use technology that moves fast (as in graphic design).

But for parents who have already fallen out of work, Mattison suggests you have nothing to lose by trying unconventional ways of negotiating your way back. 'There have been quite a few women who have done what I would call very senior work experience,' she says. 'Find a business you'd absolutely love to work in, go and do three months there and be indispensable, and you may just find you get hired on your own terms. You can do that when you're not replacing a salary.' Mature interns are also old enough to have friends and acquaintances in senior positions who might smooth their path. The mature internships organised at a raft of companies by the women's magazine *Red* are almost certainly a pilot scheme worth expanding.

And while outright aggression in negotiations rarely pays off, the mistake many parents make is to fold too quickly: to retreat at the first 'no', rather than arguing their corner and producing supporting evidence (some of which can be usefully trawled from the next chapter of this book). Sometimes it just takes a bit of chutzpah. Tim hid his four-day week from his clients originally but has got bolder about negotiating it now: 'I've found that you have to be quite bolshy about it. A lot of people just don't think it's an option.'

It's hard to feel bolshy when you are still leaking milk under your work blouse, of course, or when the whole family depends on you keeping your job. But it's not hard, in these vulnerable circumstances, to feel angry and disillusioned: and that anger can serve a working parent well. The key to a Z-shaped career is being able to think very differently, and a lot less loyally, about work.

Perhaps the single best piece of advice I heard while writing this book came from the headhunter Deborah Loudon, and it was to remember that organisations are ungrateful places. Loyalty is rarely returned in full, and certainly not for ever, yet women in particular tend to suffer from what Americans call 'Princess Syndrome': the belief that if you do your job well enough and wait long enough, someone will 'rescue' you with promotion or a pay rise. This is a risky strategy even if you intend to spend a lifetime with one company, but near-suicidal if you plan to move, since you may not be visible to headhunters or to rivals. And it contributes to what Loudon describes as one of the great career mistakes: staying past the point where you could have jumped into something better.

Charles Russam runs the recruitment agency Russam GMS, which specialises in placing interim managers. The mark of a good interim, he argues, is that while they often move on to a client's permanent payroll eventually, they won't behave like an employee. 'If you meet an interim, after 20 seconds they've found out what you do and they are looking for opportunities,' he says. 'When they are in a position they think like a business proprietor: they're cautious about doing things that cost a lot of money, they're always looking for ways of doing things differently. Their view will be "this might go on for three or four years and then the whole cycle starts again".' And that's a very useful mindset for any working parent, since in a a successful zigzag career you need to know exactly when to cut your losses and run.

The very best managers do painstakingly develop and mentor talent throughout life's ups and downs: I've worked for three men over my career without whom I would not be where I am now. But they were, frankly, exceptions to the rule. The reality is that managers are often too busy with today's crisis to worry about tomorrow, as the management consultants McKinsey discovered when they recently examined why companies still weren't spending enough time identifying future stars, despite years of arguing that nurturing talent should be a company's single biggest priority. 'Talent management puts you under strain because it stops you from doing what you are rewarded for,' as one senior executive bluntly put it.[8] And that, in short, is why it isn't safe to leave your career in someone else's hands.

For a successful Z-shaped career, you have to stop thinking like an employee, and start thinking like a brand. This is, admittedly, the kind of phrase that puts right-thinking people's teeth on edge. But it simply means thinking of yourself not as a job title, but as a bundle of skills and experiences and contacts which could be channelled into all sorts of different things, and then identifying what distinguishes you from other brands on offer: are you quicker, sharper, more creative, better with people? Brands stand out in a cluttered market by being sharply defined: and so long as they don't change those defined strengths and values, they can perfectly easily change owners. Brands adapt to changing times, but do so gradually and logically, always referring back to their origins so as to inspire trust. Brands are consistent but versatile; they can be exploited in many different ways. 'The important thing is to be very good at something, and then to have the imagination to say "But if I unpick it what are the skills that I've got?"' as Loudon puts it.

After fifteen years as a journalist, my professional identity had been as unexamined to me as breathing: it was just what I did, and after nine years at the same paper it was hard to imagine ever doing it very differently – or doing it for anyone else. It wasn't until I took a friend's advice to break my job down into its component parts – writing, analysing complex information quickly, interviewing, public speaking, understanding the machinery of government and the process of policy-making, managing and commissioning people – that it began to seem surprisingly versatile. And if the idea of creating a professional brand still feels too hideously un-British, remember Google has probably already done it for you. Even if all that comes up when you search your own name online is a dubious selection of Facebook photos, then, like it or not, you have a brand to a prospective employer. This is an excellent lesson in the importance of mastering social media before it masters you.

As a cowardly technophobe, I was horrified when my old newspaper opened an account for me on the social media site Twitter nearly three years ago. But it turned out to be a critical way of allowing me to create a professional identity that outlasted the job, to get commissioned for new work, and to maintain a voice I might otherwise have lost in my old world (since most politicians and journalists now tweet) – as well as helping me work out who on earth I was, now that I wasn't the professional person I had always been.

The American social media practitioner Rachel Happe argues that social media can also help circumvent traditional office politics because of the transparency they offer. Promoting your work and ideas via social networks makes it possible to 'own' and take credit for your efforts, which helps build a brand outside the traditional corporate hierarchy; and social networks also benefit those who can forge alliances in a feminised world, with Twitter and Facebook both used more by women than by men.

Web traffic is increasingly driven by Twitter, so it's invaluable for any small business with an online presence: recruitment agencies now trawl social media heavily for potential candidates, while nearly four in ten senior managers regularly check their Twitter feed and over six in ten regularly check the business networking site LinkedIn.[9] There is literally no easier way to create a professional brand; and since the generation now entering the workforce have essentially been self-branding since childhood via Facebook – choosing which photos to post, updating their 'status', picking who to accept or pursue as friends – it can only become more widespread.

But the real reason social media matters is that it's fast becoming to the parent what going to the pub at the end of the working day is to the childfree: somewhere to hang out and get to know people, only with a vastly bigger potential pool of connections than would ever be possible in a pub. In other words, the 'after-work economy' of informal drinks and dinners from which parents are often excluded, if they want to get home for children's bedtime, is shifting online. If many of the parents I interviewed who had left conventional office jobs were already dabbling in Twitter, Facebook or LinkedIn to stay connected to their professional worlds, the generation of digital natives coming up behind us is likely to exploit their potential to the full.

So my advice to those considering becoming parents soon is not only to 'waste' considerably more time online, but to stuff corporate loyalty, and pick opportunities to shine outside your company rather than inside it – whether virtually or in the real world. Speak at conferences or write for trade journals, join professional networks (online or otherwise) rather than internal ones, take on voluntary work if it helps to build and protect a reputation. The more connections you make, the more likely it is that one of them will one day lead to something new and interesting.

For behaving like a brand rather than an employee involves more than nauseating self-promotion. It's about maintaining the emotional distance from work to keep moving on, rather than simply falling in with the company's plans (or, as the McKinsey survey suggests, lack of them) for you. And this distance represents a serious potential problem for thoughtful employers.

When Gallup brought together data from 26 countries in 2009, it found companies with above averagely good employee engagement – basically, those whose staff were confident that the boss was looking out for their best interests and were willing to go the extra mile – performed twice as well as the rest on measures from profitability and productivity to safety incidents at work. Happier employees are, bluntly speaking, worth more money.[10] Although employees who feel resentful and unappreciated can certainly be made to clock up a certain number of hours, they are unlikely to be producing their best work while doing so. Like 1930s movie stars, keeping one foot chastely on the floor in every passionate bedroom scene, they're going accurately through the motions but their hearts aren't in it – and that is not likely to change until the cause of their resentment is tackled. When employees stop thinking like old-fashioned employees, it's time for bosses to stop thinking like old-fashioned bosses too.

8

TIME FOR A CHANGE

There is a story told about the first women to forge careers as ground crew in the American air force which sums up for me the way change can spread through working life.[1] When female engineers first began working in numbers on the flight lines in the 1960s, they were given the same heavy toolboxes to carry as the men. But within a few days, the men began to notice a sound they weren't used to. Closer inspection revealed the women had fixed skate wheels to their toolboxes to make them easier to pull around.

The men all laughed at them, but within a few months all the toolboxes were miraculously on wheels. What was initially seen as a sign of the women's weakness became accepted as a practical solution to a problem about which men had, until then, presumably merely grumbled. Women were the catalyst for change because the heavy toolboxes were a bigger nuisance for them but also because, coming fresh to the job, they simply didn't accept it was the way things had to be – and they stumbled on an answer that made everyone more, not less, efficient.

The whole panoply of what is formally called flexible work – part-time jobs, working from home, term-time working around school holidays, compressed and annualised hours, flexitime, sabbaticals – is still commonly seen as a concession to women's 'weakness', or desire actually to see their children grow up. But the recession arguably marks the first time this 'weakness' has been widely seen not as part of the problem for corporate Britain, but as a solution. Factories have always cut hours when business was slow, but this time the professions have followed suit, with eight out of ten companies at the height of the recession either already increasing or planning to increase the availability of part-time roles to help cut their costs.[2] The recession offers some extremely useful lessons about who really wants more time, and how to give it to them.

The textbook example is the accountancy giant KPMG, which introduced its Flexible Futures programme in 2009 as a temporary measure to avoid job losses in the wake of the City meltdown. Staff could either volunteer to work one day a week less (and lose a day's pay) or take a three-month sabbatical on 30 per cent of salary. KPMG had long had a history of being open to flexible working, but this was an unusually 'virtuous' form of it: staff could be confident their careers wouldn't be harmed by taking time out, and could actively feel they were doing the company good, by saving jobs. (They also knew they would be back on full salary before long.) The stigma of part-time working was removed, leaving only one question: do you want more time, or more money? Put this way, 86 per cent of the staff volunteered for Flexible Futures, about four times more than could ultimately be accepted and nearly ten times the number who normally work flexibly at the firm.

And in a company where the male to female ratio is roughly half and half, that means a critical mass of men volunteering to cut their hours for the first time. It's an extremely interesting answer to the question of what men would do if they didn't feel they would be punished for taking their lives back. When the company axed its emergency programme a year later, not everybody opted to go back to their old hours – an indication that it had tapped into an unmet need. 'We did find some people went on the programme and decided that actually they quite liked it, and requested to go part-time or change their hours in some way,' says a spokesman. 'We were already, and continue to be, very keen on flexible working.'

There is a harder lesson to be learned from the KPMG experience too, and it's about why the part-time jobs that employers want to offer don't always match the parents who want to take them. Swamped as it was with volunteers, KPMG accepted first those who suited its business needs: you were more likely to be accepted if you worked in a department hard hit by the City crash than if you specialised in insolvency, say. And that is a wake-up call for anyone who thinks that tugging on employers' heartstrings, demanding that they recognise the emotional and social damage caused by long hours, will magically unleash more flexible jobs and so allow more parents to pursue a Z-shaped career without having to leap out of conventional companies. Dramatic changes in working life are driven by the balance sheet – and if more parents want to claw back those one or two days a week that make a difference to family life, they'll have to demonstrate a hard economic case for creating the jobs that allow them to do so. We need to ditch that horribly twee phrase, 'family-friendly' working, and start talking about smart working instead – which means exploring both how parents can move towards the 'half a wife' model, and what employers could gain from it too.

That means more than explaining how and why changing working patterns can slash head office costs, boost productivity and reach untapped talent in good times as well as bad: it's not enough to show that change can be profitable. It means showing that *not* changing also has a cost, and that it has become too risky to rely on perpetual presence and long hours as the measure of a 'good' employee and the route to commercial success.

One critical reason for managers turning down requests to work from home is a deep-seated belief that, as an employer of several hundred people once disarmingly told me, 'I just don't think people work *properly* when they work from home.' Outside his office, rows of people tapped industriously away on computers: it is doubtless as soothing a sight now as it was 200 years ago, when a hawk-eyed factory owner could look out onto the floor and literally watch the product taking shape under his staff's busy hands. But a twenty-first-century employer gazing contentedly upon his staff can no longer be entirely confident of what he sees. How many of those people, sitting virtuously at their keyboards, are really doing the Ocado order or emailing their girlfriends? The belief that bums on seats equals profitability is as hopelessly ill adapted to computerised, knowledge-based industries as horses were to warfare in the age of the tank. Commercial success depends on changing your ideas, and your practices, when the world changes around you.

Somewhere in the archive vaults at British Telecom's research and development base in deepest Suffolk sits a rather eccentric little film, made and acted by a group of employees way back in 1968. Entitled *Technology in the Nineties*, it represents their best guess then at what life would be like three decades into the future: and while some of it belongs in the land of science fiction, some of it was remarkably prescient. Their imaginary Nineties people zap data and pictures to each other, for example, long before email or text messaging was ever conceived – although admittedly, they do it via elegant teak cabinets rather than smartphones. And as BT's Head of People Practice Dennis Gissing explains, the film ends with 'this guy at the dining room table with the kids running round him, working, and it says "In the future, people even work from home!" in a jokey kind of way. But you could say we were seeing it as far back as 1968. We embarked on a journey because of the technology, exploring the technology.' It's taken them a surprisingly long way.

Today 70 per cent of BT employees have some kind of flexible working: working from home, part-time, job-sharing or other kinds of flexible shift. Gissing's own team are scattered across Britain, from Scotland to the south coast, communicating with each other mostly by phone and email and occasionally gathering for team meetings. While other firms are moving their call centres abroad, BT is experimenting with 'homeshoring', or moving call centre workers back into their own homes where they can be linked up to customers' calls via remote technology. Anybody can formally request flexible working, so it isn't limited to parents and carers, and some of it is decidedly informal. Sales staff who travel frequently aren't expected to come back into the office after appointments to do their paperwork, but can do it from home, from Starbucks or from wherever they like.

The next leap forward, Gissing suggests, could be to try and understand better how work flows and match individuals' time more closely to it. 'In winter, for example, in bad weather there's more maintenance work to be done and not so much in summer. If you really got to understand the peaks and troughs in demand for your labour I think you could potentially design a contract that says "I work 50 hours a week from November to May and then I go down to less in summer".' It would cut the company's costs, but could also expand the availability of annualised hours, one of the 'full pay' options that fathers prefer. (Something similar lies behind the American trend for 'summer hours', now adopted in several British companies, where staff either get Fridays off altogether during the slower holiday months or work slightly longer hours Monday to Thursday and then clock off on Friday lunchtime.)

What is particularly interesting about BT is that men outnumber women almost four to one among its staff, showing that flexible working does indeed appeal to fathers when it's offered in a way with which they feel comfortable and when it doesn't appear to threaten their progress. The culture is set right from the top in BT: its poster boy for flexible working is a vice president, Chris Ainslie (now managing director of its regional government practice), who is a father of three. Having worked extreme hours in his previous career, Ainslie started to rethink his priorities after his twin brother died, and when he was headhunted by BT, he made a four-day week (doing compressed hours) a condition of joining.[3]

A more typical scenario at BT is the man working from home, who takes time out to do the school runs and bath his children, before working later at night to finish off. He might not be reachable for an hour or so in the early evening (although previously, he might have been stuck on the Tube, equally unreachable) but he's using the hours once wasted commuting to create 'wife time'. These are relatively small changes, but they can make all the difference, says Gissing: 'A while ago we had a case where the guy said that with the first child he missed its first word, the first steps. He would get home and his wife said "oh, this happened today". With the second child he was *there* when all those things happened. And you are only here once.'

The reason BT is so far ahead of corporate Britain in implementing home working is that it started experimenting with it back in the 1980s, not from a romantic belief in the sanctity of family life but from an unabashed commercial desire to demonstrate confidence in its wares and dream up new uses for them. Technology companies increasingly dominate the 'best companies for working mothers' league tables thanks to their enthusiasm for home working, which partly reflects a natural confidence in the kit: they were well placed to see the revolutionary potential of moving away from storing electronic documents on individual computer hard drives (so you have to be at your desk to read them) and towards storing data remotely 'in the cloud', accessible from anywhere. But as Maggie Berry of the industry network Women in Technology points out, they are also driven by a new understanding of how much it costs to keep people at a desk for 12 hours a day.

Office life as we know it is expensive, and getting more so: at a time of dwindling oil supplies and growing concern over global warming, it beggars belief that companies are still carrying the considerable costs of keeping expensive city centre buildings heated, lit and serviced for people who could actually be working from home instead. BT estimates it saved a staggering £500 million on office costs by letting more of its staff telework – basing themselves either at home or in dedicated local offices much closer to their homes – while cutting its energy usage by a fifth.[4] It's a greener, leaner case for flexible working that is not yet widely made but should become ever more attractive to companies as pressure on balance sheets grows.

Teleworking can also allow smaller companies to expand without having to rent more square footage; converting valued staff into teleworkers can avoid a painful exodus of talent for a company that has to relocate. Maggie, a single parent, quit her full-time job when her company moved its headquarters. 'It was an hour and a half commute, three hours a day in the car . . . it wouldn't have worked with any kind of family life. The truth is most of the men at senior executive levels shipped the family out there to live, and their wives didn't work.' But why couldn't she have been offered the chance to work partly from home? It is astonishing that the government's official advice on relocation (through the widely used website BusinessLink) doesn't promote teleworking, merely offers an expensive list of bribes to encourage staff to move. But it's madness to waste thousands paying key workers' mortgages if you could get them to work at home for free.

Flexible working can be a powerful recruiting tool, particularly for small firms seeking to punch above their weight by hiring the kind of talent they might not normally attract. Neil, a former senior civil servant, took his current management role with a charity because, as he says, 'I wanted not to get completely out [of government circles] – I'm still in touch with some of the same people – but to do something where I could get a little more order in my life and see the kids while they were growing up.' The attraction was not just more regular office hours, but a deal to work from home on Fridays: 'Now I do breakfast, and two days a week I walk my eldest down to school. On Friday mornings, they do reading for half an hour with mums and dads at his school, so I can do that and then I work at home and pick him up at 3.15.' His new hours are an excellent example of how one partner's working life can determine the other's: before, his wife Anna was at home full-time with their two boys, since someone had to hold the fort because of his long hours and extensive travel. But when Neil changed jobs she finally felt able to go back to work four days a week, doing compressed hours. Between her day off, and the extra time he has gained, they have the 'wife time' they needed.

Yet the big prize for employers is perhaps the least expected one. Far from turning staff into slackers slumped in front of daytime television, teleworking seems to boost productivity (BT's rose by 20 per cent as it rolled out flexible working between 2001 and 2007). The US-based Telework Research Network calculates that corporate America could save $400 billion if everyone who could telework did so for half the week, and most of that estimated saving comes not from cheaper electricity bills but from rising productivity. American Express found its teleworkers generated nearly half as much business again as those stuck in the office.[5] It's surprising what you can do when freed from constant distraction and interruption – by gossipy colleagues, and too often by managers themselves. It's easy to interrupt someone you can see across the office with a pointless quibble, or drag them into a meeting; if you have to pick up the phone, you'll tend to do so only when it matters.

Modern companies already know that a domestic vibe can encourage creativity and therefore productivity: it's why they spend a small fortune trying to recreate an ersatz feeling of home in the office, installing comfy sofas, free espresso machines, even in-house gyms and bars. According to research by the architecture practice Gensler,[6] 22 per cent of managers have their best ideas at home, when they're relaxed enough to let their minds play freely. If so, it should be cheaper to design workers back into the home than to rebuild home piece by piece in the office. The same Gensler study found that managers spent over half their time at their desks, a quarter of it in meetings – probably the only time when they needed to bounce ideas off other people – and the rest offsite. Shrinking the fancy office, redrawing the meeting schedule and letting more staff do their deskwork from the kitchen table could be, quite literally, the most productive solution – as an even more radical experiment at the American retail giant Best Buy suggests.

Born out of despair at the company's workaholic culture, it began as a small and secretive programme of radical change in one extremely stressed department at the company's corporate headquarters. Meetings were cancelled, schedules ripped up, and staff told they didn't have to be in the office at any set time: it was fine to leave at 2.30 and collect the kids from school, or even go fishing and roll in at lunchtime, so long as the work got done. Essentially, staff could do what they liked from where they liked, so long as they met their targets. The golden rule was not to do anything that wasted individuals' time, the company's time or the customers' money.

The two HR executives behind it, Jody Thompson and Cali Ressler, didn't tell their chief executive what they were doing; they felt it was too likely to be stamped on from above. So the programme spread by word of mouth among managers. By the time the chief executive found out two years later exactly what was going on, it had proved itself: productivity rose by up to 35 per cent in departments using the so-called 'Results Orientated Work Environment', or ROWE for short.[7]

It wasn't an easy process, especially for older employees who had already given their family life to the company and were now effectively being told those sacrifices had been pointless and unnecessary. Some managers fought it, and so did some employees (Ressler and Thompson have since moved on to start their own consultancy). But the basic philosophy of setting workers free is spreading.

The American company Netflix, a virtual video store which sends DVDs by post to subscribers, has scrapped holiday entitlement and just lets staff take as much time off as they like. 'Rules and policies and regulations and stipulations are innovation killers. People do their best work when they're unencumbered,' as their vice president for corporate communication, Steve Swasey, put it.[8] Netflix pushed up its revenue by a third last year.

It's not as delightfully laid-back as it sounds, of course. Netflix weeds out those who don't hit performance targets, so its staff are presumably motivated not to be away for too long: they're effectively policing themselves, instead of being policed by managers. Badly delivered, schemes like this could even encourage the old arms race in hours, since it's human nature to look nervously over your shoulder at how much time everyone else is taking off and try to take less. But introduced sensitively, managing by results rather than effort can work for both parents and their bosses.

It's an undeniable leap of faith for an employer to accept that they might only see someone they rely on twice a week, just as that person must trust both ambitious colleagues and supervisors not to undermine them on the days they're not in. But it's a skill many managers are having to learn anyway, thanks to the rapid growth of outsourcing, or the controversial practice of farming out routine tasks overseas. Most of us are used to ringing the bank and being rerouted to a call centre in Delhi, but the same cost-cutting practice is spreading quietly through professions from accountancy to architecture: London-based law firms now regularly send routine legal work to highly qualified, English-speaking but proportionately cheaper lawyers operating remotely from Mumbai. It's done nothing for British job security, but the silver lining is that managers are learning to supervise workforces thousands of miles away, by email and Skype and phone, without ever meeting them face to face. And as Maggie Berry points out, these are exactly the same skills needed to manage Britons working from home. If you can send case files to Bangalore, your staff can surely read them at home in Basingstoke; and if you already work across three time zones, would it really kill you to let someone start and finish an hour early?

Managing like this does require a different way of thinking, a focus on measuring the results that come out of a working day rather than the time that goes into it. But it's the results produced, not the time expended, that make money for companies. BT managers are trained to set very careful targets for individual employees, on the basis that if the work gets done, managers can be reasonably sure they're working properly wherever they are.

'If you give people certain responsibilities and objectives and deliverables, then the question is, are they delivering – are they on the calls they need to be on, or getting to the customer at the right time?' says Gissing. 'If they do, I don't mind if they start work at 7 a.m. so they can go to Tesco's later when it's quiet, or go and see their ageing mum, or even watch Richard and Judy before they start working. If you have an important meeting on a Monday morning, you have to arrange things around that, of course. But it has to come down to trust: I honestly think most people want to do a good job.' Those who don't are likely to miss their targets and can be performance-managed in the normal way.

Managing like this is tougher than sticking stubbornly to a conventional timetable, not least because it requires being constantly open to change. It takes imagination, lateral thinking, and a really good understanding of what is going on under the bonnet. Managers need to know exactly which tasks add value – which meetings, for example, are important enough that a homeworker should come in for them – and be able to quantify things that are sometimes hard to pin down, such as what a worker should have achieved within a given day. It's much easier simply to tick a time sheet. But I suspect one of the reasons that productivity rises in around six in ten small to medium companies that introduce flexibility[9] is that these companies are being managed more smartly and imaginatively as a result of introducing flexibility – although no doubt it helps that their employees are grateful, and now less likely to have to throw a sickie just to take a child to the GP. (On which well-worn subject, incidentally, while women do on average take more days off than men, it's workers in their early twenties who call in sick more than any other age group. They may well have been up all night, but probably not with a toddler.) Demanding that everyone stick to traditionally macho long hours can be a sign not of a lean and mean management operation, but of a rather lazy or flabby one.

After all, if long hours were everything, South Korea would rule the world: its people work on average 44 hours a week and until 2004 it was routine only to have Sunday off, yet the country lags well behind America and Europe in the amount of goods, services and wealth churned out in that time. (And its exhausted citizens have so few children that it's on the verge of a demographic crisis.) As anyone who has ever sat at a desk for so long they can't think straight will know, productivity is undermined by fatigue, boredom and resentment. The West is not going to win a race to the bottom on working hours against young and highly populous emerging nations, whatever the steel magnate Ratan Tata's views on his British managers' willingness to go the extra mile, so we are going to have to compete more cunningly on creativity and innovation instead. That means increasing productivity by working not more, but smarter.

Over the last four decades, the surge of mothers into work has helped Western economies grow, as women contributed literally billions more hours to the work effort. There's still more to do to ensure that parents can return to work if they want to after a career break or redundancy, and some intriguing opportunities to bring in people currently stuck outside the labour market, although the pool of talent to be tapped in this way is now starting to shrink. But the next great leap of growth will probably come less from adding hours than from getting more out of those hours, and exploiting unused talents in people who are already working – frazzled young parents who could be stopped from dropping out, with a little rejigging of the job; the 45 per cent of part-timers working below the level for which they're qualified, often because they can't get the hours they need in more senior roles or have been essentially put out to grass;[10] and people approaching retirement, who could be persuaded to stay on by a juicy part-time role. For working parents aren't alone in rebelling against the conventional working day; we're squashed happily in the middle of a multi-generational movement for change.

Marching in front of us is the 17-million-strong cohort of baby boomers now nearing retirement, many of whom no longer want to work at full stretch but can't afford to stop completely: they need imaginative part-time jobs at a senior level, which allow for a slow fade rather than a sharp drop out of work. Coming up behind us, meanwhile, are Generations Y and Z (those now respectively starting their first jobs, and leaving school). Their stereotypical image as laid-back slackers may be unfair, but the early evidence is that this generation still sets much greater store by being able to take time out than their parents did: even those graduating into the hostile jobs market of 2010 still felt work–life balance mattered more than salary in choosing a career,[11] and perhaps most strikingly of all, a third of male graduates said becoming a househusband was as potentially appealing as a job. It's no longer hard to see why the welfare minister Maria Miller said last year that flexible working was 'something most people will want to consider at some point in their working life',[12] but what many of us don't realise is that employers have an extremely pressing reason to meet us halfway. This year, the number of people turning 65 will be a staggering 22 per cent higher than in 2011[13] as the first of the post-war baby boomers reach pensionable age. We are teetering on the edge of a 'retirement cliff', a senior brain drain as millions of experienced people leave work; and because the birth cohorts following behind them are smaller, there simply aren't enough rising stars to fill the emptying desks. We are now entering the storm described nearly fifteen years ago in *The War for Talent* (1997) a landmark report from the management consultants McKinsey which argued that ageing populations would make it harder for companies to find and keep good people. In theory, parents are entering a seller's market, where the health of the economy relies on fewer of us quitting work.

As we saw in the last chapter, in practice managers are often too busy just getting through the day to think in such strategic terms. But there are simple, quick, practical steps employers could be taking to prevent talent slipping through their hands.

When Colette left her managerial job in the car industry, which involved long hours and extensive travel, she didn't even ask her boss about alternative options because 'I didn't see how it could really have been amended to a part-time role.' Yet after she left, it turns out, the job was split between two people, a reflection of just how much she had been taking on. She was surprised when I asked why it couldn't just have been split for her. 'I hadn't really thought about that. I just assumed it was because after you have been in a role for a few years you take on more things and when someone more objective has to write a job description there's no way you can cram it all into one.' Exhausted and emotionally torn, parents on the verge of resigning aren't always best placed to see alternative options, but surprisingly few of those I interviewed were asked when they quit how the company could change their mind, or even why they were going. It reflects an odd lack of curiosity, but then perhaps sometimes it's easier to tell yourself that it's 'natural' for new mothers to stop work than to wonder whether it's your fault.

Niamh O'Keeffe is a career coach, whose company First100 creates plans for a senior executive's first hundred days in the role. She increasingly works with women returning from maternity leave, and says it can be fatally convenient for both sides not to 'see' a problem: 'Women come back all gung ho and it's very difficult, but they pretend it isn't. They go on for three or six months crying in the bathroom and putting a brave face on it and then they start hatching their plans around how they are going to leave – but they want to wait a year, because they don't want it to be seen to be about the baby.

'[The woman] will do everything possible to disguise that, and nobody wants to hear that. It totally lets employers off the hook.' The parent needn't admit to having 'failed' and the employer needn't confront anything inconvenient about their working practices – so then it happens all over again with the next rising star.

Confidential exit interviews to establish why staff leave are standard practice in large firms, but perhaps the single easiest change employers could make would be not to take a resignation lying down. When good people go, it should be routine to ask if flexibility might make them stay – and perhaps especially with men, who may be leaving because they're sick of never seeing their children but would rather die than say so. While it's rare now to find a company that does not offer, in theory, some kind of flexible working, only a third of companies actively promote it to staff;[14] yet fathers, in particular, need to be actively encouraged to ask for it before they will feel safe to do so.

And while many enlightened firms now measure the progress of women through their ranks, tracking the effect of motherhood on careers, we know next to nothing about what happens to working fathers who change their hours. Is it only men with a certain view of parenthood who get to the top, too? Companies should consider identifying at least internally, and for preference in their annual reports, both the most senior level at which flexible working arrangements are active for both sexes (for example, middle or senior management) and annual staff turnover broken down by gender, since men may be more likely to leave rather than challenge long working hours.

Even once staff have left, it isn't necessarily too late. As we saw earlier, forging a successful zigzag career ideally means staying in the game throughout the life cycle, even if it's only one day a week. But life isn't always ideal, and for those who can't manage that, finding ways to make profitable use of even the smallest scraps of working time is in everyone's interests.

Slivers of Time is a not-for-profit online business, set up by a former BBC producer, which aims to match people who want to work just a few hours a week with 'mini-jobs'. It's heavily used by parents who may have had long career breaks, the long-term sick whose fitness to work might vary day by day, carers trying to fit in a little work around the unpredictable needs of disabled relatives, and increasingly by shift workers seeking to pick up a few extra hours (Tesco now uses it to distribute extra shifts at busy times).

'It's enabled people to get back into the workplace who are clearly bright and willing to work but have been compromised by traditional rostering systems,' says Claire Madden, business development manager at Slivers of Time. 'For some people it'll be that short-term stepping stone but others I think have a way of life which means they are always going to need that flexibility, perhaps a child with a learning difficulty. What's important is that companies are beginning to realise they can still use these people.'

These bite-sized nuggets of work are controversial: the last government halted moves towards a 'slivers of time' model after protests that it should be finding proper jobs for people, not a few unreliable hours a week. Mini-jobs tend to be low-paid and not especially high-skilled, such as care work, manual labouring, or catering. But a recent report from the anti-poverty charity the

Joseph Rowntree Foundation, carried out jointly with the single parents' organisation Gingerbread and the Institute for Fiscal Studies, suggested slivers of working time could both meet a strong desire among lone parents not to do more than two days a week and help the long-term unemployed back into work.

However, the big prize in productivity terms, and the one with greatest potential to reduce wastage for employers, is cracking the hardest part of a zigzag career: getting back on track after a sideways move. This is where frustration and despair sets in for parents, and it's where money leaks out for companies who invest thousands in training and developing staff only for them to vanish on to the 'mommy track' to oblivion. Sometimes they are sidelined deliberately, by managers who don't see parents as promotion material; but sometimes it's a more benign kind of neglect. Niamh O'Keeffe says she has seen too many well-intentioned companies 'patronise the maternity returner, letting them come back and sit on the bench' when they return on a three-day week, when all that does is erode confidence. Well-meaning managers assume that a new parent won't want to take on anything challenging. After a year or two of being passed over like this, parents lose faith in their abilities, and after a year or two more their managers have forgotten what those parents could once do.

Working out when to re-enter the fray in a competitive industry after taking a career break is rather like playing one of those mass playground skipping games beloved of small girls: you have to judge the speed at which the rope is turning accurately in order to jump back in without tripping over everyone else, and the longer you are out the harder it is to get your timing right. Sometimes what's needed is a nudge.

Two years ago, the 'magic circle' law firm Allen & Overy broke new ground by announcing that its full equity partners – those senior lawyers granted a stake in the business, and access to the big money – would henceforth be allowed to work part-time or to take 52 days extra a year to cover school holidays, in the hope of drawing more women into the partnership.

This wasn't, however, just any old part-time: partners are not allowed to do less than the magic four days, and critically only for five years, after which the arrangement will be reviewed. Lawyers taking this deal are being invited to see it as a temporary fix, not a lifestyle choice. The expectation is that they will ultimately be back competing on conventional terms. Is that cruel? Or is it being cruel to be kind?

Nobody wants to feel pressured into longer days before they are ready, and deadlines are difficult for any parent who still wants more children. Yet on the whole I think setting an annual review on flexible working arrangements – so that every year, you discuss with your manager whether to carry on or increase your hours – makes sense, if it's sensitively done (and it can be done under the existing law). It wouldn't mean parents being forced, Cinderella-like, to snap back on the stroke of midnight; if a parent formally requests and gets reduced hours, those hours can't legally be changed back without their consent. But making both sides stop and think, once a year, about whether they've fallen into a rut could prevent the killing of careers with kindness. It could also prompt employers to think much more deeply about what they have to offer good people who want to keep moving up the ladder, without necessarily going back to working 50 hours a week.

Parents need to be realistic about the limits on playing with the working day, of course: setting workers free from their desks makes sense in 'knowledge economy' jobs when you are buying someone's ideas, but less so in a biscuit factory, where it's all about getting shortbread in a tin by 5 p.m. There are still plenty of jobs, from policing to emptying dustbins, for which you just have to be there – or where eye contact, touch, the bodily reassurance of another person, matter. One in ten GP consultations may now be by phone, but nobody wants to get a cancer diagnosis this way.

And although both biscuit packers and GPs can easily work three days a week, the factory manager can't if she is the only person who can decide when to halt production. Part-time is difficult for those with very specialist skills or anyone at the end of a decision-making chain, since decisions can't always wait until Monday: there *is* a 'missing half' to some part-time jobs, a body of work that doesn't get done when you are not in the office, and employers are entitled to worry about it.

This doesn't mean admitting defeat so much as picking the right kind of flexibility for the job. There is a rare form of working time that is more common in the private sector than the public, and more widely granted at senior level than among juniors, which suggests it can be a very good way indeed to wangle a three-day week without sliding backwards: it is the most under-exploited form of flexible working, with half of workers thinking their job could be done in this way although they don't currently have the option.[15] Why isn't job-sharing more popular?

Headhunters have a vested interest in not pushing job-shares, since they usually get the same fee for finding two sharers as for finding one full-timer, even though it's twice the effort. Employers may also worry about what will happen if one half of a share thrives and the other doesn't. But buying two brains for the price of one can be a bargain. One study found most senior level job-share partnerships were up to 30 per cent more productive than one person working alone,[16] while many sharers say bouncing ideas off each other encourages risk-taking and creativity. It's also a neat solution to jobs that demand more hours than seems fair for one person to give. 'I think we should be seriously revisiting job-share given we don't seem to be cracking the problem of work intensification,' says Sarah Jackson, of Working Families. 'People who are doing senior roles in large organisations, actually even in small organisations, are working themselves into the ground. If you look at these extreme jobs, 70 hours a week, they should be done by two people.'

And these jobs don't even have to be shared across a working week. The husband-and-wife British diplomats Carolyn Davidson and Tom Carter became the Foreign Office's first job-sharing overseas head of mission in 2008, as joint High Commissioner for Zambia: they take turns heading the embassy or being at home looking after their two young sons. They alternate every four months so that one spouse is always in post, arguing that they're both highly focused during their working stints and refreshed by their parenting stints – although perhaps inevitably there is a subtle difference in the way they are treated. Carter says that when it's his turn at home 'I get asked all the time what it is I spend my time doing when I'm not in the office, whereas Carolyn interestingly doesn't.'[17] Nonetheless they are an excellent example of how both job-sharing (and the 'consecutive wife' parenting model as described in Chapter 5, above) can work within a very traditional career structure. Last summer, the Foreign Office appointed a second husband-and-wife job-share, Jonathan Aves and Katherine Leach, as ambassador to Armenia.

For those not lucky enough to have married one, however, the biggest hurdle to job-sharing is finding a suitable professional 'other half'. And here a relatively simple idea could make a difference. When Treasury civil servant Jonathan Lepper needed a transplant operation, the brush with mortality made him rethink his life and in particular the time he spent with his children. He decided he wanted to return to work as a job-share, but didn't know where to find a partner. Out of Lepper's frustration came the idea of a Civil-Service-wide online job board, through which any Whitehall employee could seek like-minded sharers: it went live in 2009 with the personal backing of the head of the Civil Service, Cabinet Secretary Gus O'Donnell, who publicly urged more men to try it. He had, he said, personal regrets about having taken a job as John Major's press secretary – perhaps the most extreme of extreme jobs – when his daughter was born, and effectively leaving his wife to do the parenting.[18] There is no reason why other big public sector organisations, unions, professional bodies and multinational companies couldn't set up similar 'job-share dating' agencies for their people, too – and it needn't stop there.

The business networking site LinkedIn, which allows people to post a professional profile and CV online, enables users to tart around discreetly for job offers by clicking a button to express interest in 'new career opportunities'. Adding a button for 'interested in job-sharing' would at a stroke let them search quickly and discreetly for potential partners among 100 million registered users worldwide, and thus perhaps apply confidently for positions that were out of their reach as part-timers.

It's this ability to move on that matters. Like great white sharks, careers have to keep swimming to survive, and that means being able to switch companies, get promoted, or learn new things. But parents who have negotiated shorter hours and fear they might lose them by moving will tend to stay in jobs they've outgrown, which helps explain why part-timers are relatively badly paid. An estimated 1.25 million women in Britain who have downgraded their jobs to get shorter hours end up 'stuck',[19] working below what they're capable of – and that's just the women.

Although Women in Technology was set up primarily to encourage more women into the male-dominated world of IT,

Maggie Berry was approached recently by a father working at a senior level in technology in the City. 'He was saying "I have got a part-time role where I work a three or four day week: my wife and I both work and it suits us. But I want to move and I have nowhere to move",' she explains. Very few jobs in IT are openly advertised as part-time, and he had seen nothing at his level, even though experience had shown it was possible to do his job in this way. 'So he was asking "At what point in the interview do I say 'Oh and by the way I want to work a four-day week?'"' This father is worried that bringing up the idea of part-time work too early will make him look less 'serious' – but he can't just gamble on being able to sort something out later.

While some exemplary employers in Britain today are bending over backwards to accommodate parents, there aren't enough of them: flexible working has spread patchily, often relying on individual managers' whims. It's now far easier for parents to shrink the job they already have to fit, with the vast majority of formal flexible working requests granted. A boss who already knows how good you are may well change the job to keep you: one study found that only around 18 per cent of highly skilled women who go part-time within their existing company end up taking demotions as a result. But 41 per cent of women forced to move jobs in search of better hours slid backwards,[20] a heinous waste of talent which breaks all the rules of maximising productivity. It will always be risky for women, and rarely be appealing for men, to become a family's 'half earner' while that remains the case: which makes a flexible job market key to the success of the half a wife model (and also key to unlocking talent among the third of working age adults who have children).

The missing piece in the jigsaw is what Mattison and Stewart of Women Like Us call a genuine market in part-time jobs for both men and women: one where you can move jobs while remaining part-time just as you would while doing conventional hours, and where flexible work is openly available to new hires rather than being hidden away like a shameful secret.

In the summer of 2010 the lone parents' charity Gingerbread took a snapshot survey of job ads in the London press: just 17 per cent openly mentioned flexible working (and none at all were for job-sharers). Yet over 95 per cent of employers say they offer some kind of flexible working. Where are all these jobs hiding? Too often they're available internally and somewhat grudgingly, mostly to new mothers coming back from maternity leave, but never made public. They are being used to retain good people who might otherwise have left, but not to recruit them.

Several times while researching this book, I encountered the phenomenon of the 'invisible' flexible job: employers who were personally happy to consider job-sharers or working from home, but wouldn't say so in a job advert. Last spring, I was called by a headhunter wanting to pick my brains about potential candidates for a vacancy as CEO of a small organisation. He sent over the job spec, and it immediately became obvious that while everyone I could think of who might do it was based in London, the job was hundreds of miles away. Couldn't they consider people working remotely from home some of the week? I asked. Oh yes, came the reply. But if it doesn't say so in the job ad, nobody reading it will necessarily know.

Employers may think it doesn't need saying, but parents are reluctant to ask upfront about unconventional working patterns in case it marks them out as 'difficult', and so they look for signals that it's safe to ask. Parents miss interesting opportunities and employers lose interesting candidates because flexible jobs are not currently visible to the naked eye.

Once a company identifies someone it actively wants to poach, the competitive instinct to secure that talent before a rival does trumps concerns about working hours. Charles Russam, who runs the interim management company Russam GMS, says that most employers invariably say they need a full-timer but 'if they select the candidate they want and that interim then says "I can't really do five days, but I can do four"', most clients won't mind'. The challenge is triggering that same competitive instinct to secure talent the employer hasn't yet met.

The last government considered granting the right to request flexible working from day one in a job, rather than having to wait until you've been employed for 26 weeks, in the hope of opening up conversations at interview stage. But without a shift in the way companies think, men in particular may still not risk it. The bigger prize is to for employers to ask themselves even before they advertise a job: if my dream candidate applied, would I really mind them working a three-day week? Does this job have to be done the way it's always been done, or is it just organised that way out of habit? Too often nobody thinks to ask, new staff are hired by default on the same terms as those who left (quite possibly to see more of their children) and the cycle begins again.

One way to reset the clock would be for the government to introduce a presumption of flexibility, with a legal requirement for the public sector that all jobs should be clearly advertised as capable of being worked flexibly unless there is a good business reason why they can't be. It wouldn't mean every job *had* to be part-time, but it would mean employers at least asking themselves the question – with knock-on benefits for existing staff as it became clear which jobs could be redesigned without the sky falling in. When East Riding of Yorkshire council asked its managers to think creatively about configuring jobs before advertising them – for example, by considering whether head teachers could job-share – as part of a drive to increase flexible working at senior levels, it ended up creating around 600 new part-time jobs.[21]

There would undoubtedly be a mutiny if such a duty was applied to the private sector. But a useful compromise would be promoting the voluntary adoption by employers of a big banner stating 'We welcome flexible working applications for this job' on every advert where appropriate – with a threat that if the scheme didn't catch on voluntarily it could be legally enforced. If job recruitment sites asked every time an ad was booked whether the job was potentially flexible (and therefore eligible for the banner), then every time the HR department drew up a job spec it would need to ask the same question of the line manager – and some would begin to think 'why not?' instead of 'why should we?'. They might even begin to notice that, as the headhunter Deborah Loudon tells her clients, a juicy role advertised flexibly will draw three times as many applicants. The 'invisible' jobs that parents can't currently see or get at might finally come out of the woodwork.

But the quid pro quo is that employers are entitled to expect some help from the state in working smarter. Shortening hours is not like shortening a pair of trousers: you can't just lop some time off a job and hope it works. Converting full-time posts into part-time ones may mean moving meetings, shuffling responsibilities between colleagues, changing reporting lines. (Gissing's boss at BT, for example, is a senior director who tries to work one or two days a week from home, so she reorganises her diary to fit all her face-to-face meetings in the office time and writes her reports from home.) Job-shares also bring with them daunting questions for small businesses in particular, such as how to split the National Insurance or the company car. It's not unreasonable for employers to expect some help from the state with making these changes, given the difference they could make to the way families organise their lives.

So I would like to see a government-backed national agency set up with a brief to increase productivity by promoting smart working. It could combine timely advice on job redesign, via a helpline for small businesses, and an online forum for employers to swap advice and tips among themselves. And since making the right jobs visible to parents isn't enough, it should play a key role in making the right parents visible to employers.

Many bosses' old-fashioned idea of what a flexible worker is – someone's mum, not too bright or ambitious, keen to leave at 3.30 p.m. – bears absolutely no resemblance to the people now out there. Women Like Us has begun to change that image on a shoestring, by building an impressive database of available jobs and available workers from scratch, but they would be the first to admit it's patchy; and clients still often approach them to fill junior roles, coming back with senior roles only when they see how impressive the candidates actually are. Making the leap to a comprehensive national database (and then perhaps linking it to the national smarter working agency I've suggested, and in turn to job-share registers such as that set up by the Civil Service) will cost money that, as a social enterprise, Women Like Us doesn't currently have: and it's unlikely ever to make serious profit, because of the labour-intensive way it works with its clients. A relatively small amount of pump-priming capital from either industry or government would be an astute longer-term investment.

For there are some things only governments can really do. Sometimes only the state has the reach or the money to intervene where markets fail: sometimes only the state has a big enough overview to join all the dots. And it's the state on which we rely to settle disputes, reconcile opposing interests, and judge where the balance of power lies between individuals and business. It's the state that ultimately holds the ring in family and working life. And so we come finally to the things that only the state can do.

9

LINES OF DESIRE

Coming out of the Tube one afternoon last spring my eye was caught by an advert plastered all the way up the escalator. It was an image of two children and their parents cramped into an impossibly tight frame, with the caption 'Are you feeling hemmed in?' The small print extolled the virtues of cheap family homes within a relatively quick commute of the capital in somewhere apparently called 'north Londonshire'.

The campaign was part of a controversial attempt to rebrand Northamptonshire, never officially classed as part of the Home Counties, as an overlooked nirvana for commuters. But it was controversial for all the wrong reasons. There was some grumbling about the 'north Londonshire' tag burying the historic name of the county, some concern about the impact on locals of inviting Londoners to come and push up house prices, but few people seemed to ask the obvious question – why the hell should you have to move sixty miles, and up to three hours' daily round trip, from your job just to afford a reasonably sized house?

There is a good case to make for house prices as the hidden, unloved dictator of family life. Worldwide, shrinking birth rates are closely linked to skyrocketing real estate, with families in crowded urban Singapore, Japan and Hong Kong sometimes literally unable to afford room for more children. Here, the Conservative minister David Willetts once argued persuasively that delayed motherhood is linked to needing to save longer for a house deposit: middle-class couples like to buy before starting a family. And while one of the simplest ways for parents to see more of their children would be to shorten the journey to work, it's hard when they're being pushed further and further away from where the good jobs are, simply to afford a house. Families who cling to city centres to avoid commuting, meanwhile, are trapped into holding down two full-time jobs just to afford the mortgage.

One seemingly attractive answer is to encourage renting over buying; middle-class families do it happily in many European cities, on longer and more secure leases than are typical here. Renting is a great way for families who are still experimenting with different permutations of work and 'wife time' to avoid committing to a mortgage, but the trouble with long-term renting is that you don't build up an asset: there is nothing to sell to fund retirement, nothing to remortgage in a crisis, and smugness in a falling market gives way to chagrin in a rising one. During the two years before the market crashed in 2008, the money tied up in bricks and mortar represented nearly 40 per cent of personal wealth in this country.[1]

So this government is right to advocate a stable housing market where prices rise slowly and don't crash so sickeningly. After all, you can buy a house in Germany now for pretty much what you could in the 1970s in real terms (house prices more than doubled in real terms over the same period here), which means there is no mad rush. Parents of small children can rent, save up, and buy later when their earnings are peaking with a small mortgage to be paid off by retirement. They still have an asset, and if they don't make the same crazy profits as British homeowners in good times, nor are they so weighed down by mortgage debt that they have no money for anything else. But politicians have been rather unforthcoming about exactly how to slow the merry-go-round down to German speeds, because all the options hurt. Raising stamp duty hurts those desperate to sell, like the newly divorced; making it harder to get a mortgage freezes out first-time buyers, and clamping down on buy-to-let reduces the supply of cheap rented properties. And while building more houses so that demand more closely matches supply is one of the few positive ways to lower prices, nothing causes outrage in a pretty chocolate-box village like the rumble of the concrete mixer – even though such villages are elegantly dying all over the country because young families can't afford to move in and keep the schools and shops alive.

What has happened to house prices is an excellent example of why working parents who think Westminster politics isn't really about them are making a grave mistake. Politics is literally everywhere in family life, and public policy is the hidden hand that shapes our parenting: it's buried in pay packets and parents' evenings, in disputes at work and in the speed with which suspicious rashes do (or don't) get seen in Accident and Emergency. It's there in the bored child, doodling on the photocopying paper in the corner of Mummy's office because there is no summer holiday play scheme and there are no more favours to call in. And it's there, sometimes, in fathers creeping out of the house before their children are awake to start the long journey to work. Families don't always have time to trace the connections between distant, dull-sounding decisions and their own daily lives, but governments have no such excuse – and they must do so not just for parents' sake, but in the wider national interest too. So what I want to do here is to join up the dots between parent, grandparent, employer and the state, and show how the interests of all could best be served.

A good place to start would be by ministers publicly explaining how the property market sours family life – delaying settling down, trapping parents into working long hours at the expense of time with their children, pushing extended families apart. They might then be free to make a more credible case for carefully deflating the property bubble by building more homes, rather than letting it blow up and burst all over again: house-building is expensive, but we pay a terrible emotional price for avoiding it. At the current feeble rate of building, it's estimated that by 2026 barely a quarter of 30 to 34-year-olds will be able to afford even a purpose-built flat,[2] which suggests they will have little hope of a family house. The next step is to make the bigger connection between home and work. It's convenient proximity to work that makes big cities and their surrounding commuter belts so ludicrously expensive. But what if work could more often come to us, instead of the other way round?

Many parents dream of being able to raise children away from the pressures of the big city, in a far-flung place by the sea, and several of the parents I interviewed had used the changes in their working life to downshift somewhere idyllic; selling up in the city, and releasing capital, was also the only way some could afford to change their hours. Samantha, who was made redundant from her job in PR when she was pregnant, moved with her family to Northern Ireland when her husband was offered a job there. 'It was a stunning place to bring up kids: we lived right at the northernmost tip of County Antrim, right by the sea. We lived in a tiny basement flat in London with no garden, no natural light: here we were offered a four-bedroomed detached house with a view, by the sea.'

The price, of course, was leaving the city where she was most likely to get work. 'When I left I really, really felt like I was kissing goodbye to my career for ever. Belfast would be the nearest place I would have anything like the sort of work I do, and that was an hour and a half away. I really felt like I was burning all my bridges when it came to work, although there was so much going for us here.' Fortunately Samantha has been able to build up a freelance career, however: being able to work from home was the key both to her job prospects and to a better quality of life for the whole family. Now their two boys are both in school, the couple are actively discussing whether she might become the main breadwinner while her husband, who runs a small public sector organisation, stays at home to finish the novel he has begun writing in his spare time. 'He would love that. I feel like I owe him because he's held down a job that sustained me being at home with the kids. I could work in Tesco's if I had to, and I would rather do that than give up some connection to what he loves.'

The number of people working only or mainly from home is up 21 per cent in the last decade,[3] but it's risen by nearly half in Wales, while more than one in ten workers in the south-west are now home-based. These hotspots for home workers boast beautiful countryside and an enviably relaxed lifestyle, but few big employers beyond farming and tourism; despite the fashionable fish restaurants, Cornwall actually has the lowest wages in the UK, which means if you want well-paid work here it helps to bring it with you. Just like the coming of the railways in the late nineteenth century, fast broadband can connect far-flung areas to the money and opportunities available in big cities – and without the hassle of physically transporting people there, save for the odd meeting. That matters to governments as well as parents, because a strong and sustainable recovery will require spreading wealth and work a little wider round the country.

It's natural for work to cluster in big cities. Industries tend to huddle in one place because doing so lowers transaction costs and lets companies gain more from each other than they care to admit. In the Fleet Street of old, rival newspapers' reporters traded information in the pub; Silicon Valley's early pioneers went to the same softball games and restaurants in their spare time, sent their children to the same schools, made friends in and out of the office. In both cases it was easy for the restless to move jobs or for growing companies to hire, since the best talent was never far away.

Clusters do spin apart as ways of working change. Some banks, for example, left the City for cheaper office rents in Canary Wharf when shares began to be bought and sold by computer rather than traded face to face on the Stock Exchange. But there's a limit to how far they want to scatter, and that presents a problem for the rest of the country.

One pound in every five of our national wealth is made in London, thanks to the bubble of wealth created by the City in the boom years but also to the way it sucks in money from surrounding areas. Commuters spend much of their money near their offices, not their homes; every pair of snagged tights replaced in a lunch hour, every drink after work, is a sale not rung up in their home town. So the smart alternative to the 'north Londonshire' approach is the one some local authorities are now trying: persuading residents to spend more of their lives (and money) near home, rather than importing rich commuters who then disappear for most of the week. Companies' head offices may never move that far from the major cities, but if you didn't have to actually get into London or Edinburgh or Birmingham or Bristol every day in order to work for them, wages would be ploughed back into smaller communities (and taxpayers might have to spend rather less on maintaining road and rail for the convenience of commuters).

Individuals' energy bills rise do rise if they work from home, although the saving on rail fares, petrol, office clothes and lunches out can more than compensate – and would do so even more if train companies responded to changing patterns of commuting. (On my local intercity line it costs as much to take the rush hour train twice a week as it would to commute five days a week on an annual season ticket. The sooner overground routes adopt the Parisian-style 'carnet' tickets available on the Tube, where passengers buy tickets cheaply in bulk and use them whenever they want, the better.)

But even evangelists for home working like myself can see that not everyone wants to spend their working life cooped up in the spare bedroom.

Perfectly happy home workers still occasionally get cabin fever, need somewhere vaguely professional looking to meet clients, or want to separate the domestic and the professional a little. (It's undeniably useful being able to stuff washing silently into the tumble-dryer while taking a work call, but the rest of the family may need reminding that being at home doesn't mean you are free to run all their errands.) That's why, every few weeks, I arrange a day of meetings in London, just for a change of scene and some face-to-face contact with clients. But it's also why the idea of work hubs is important.

Hubs offer drop-in deskspace for people working outside conventional offices, as and when they need it – which might be once every few months for a meeting, or might be several times a week. But they're different from the rather soulless rent-by-the-hour hot-desks traditionally available to freelances, for they have a community aspect. They offer company, gossip, someone to spark ideas off – the water-cooler moments sorely missing outside the office. We all want someone to chat to during the working day, but they don't necessarily have to be working for the same company.

'I work so much harder at home because there are no distractions, but having said that, when you are chatting to colleagues you are sometimes sharing ideas and bouncing things off each other,' says Liz Wakeham-Jones, head of marketing research for Workhubs Network, which keeps a register of the growing number of hubs in Britain. 'You're bringing the best of both worlds together: you've got your social interaction, but you can turn it on or off as you fancy.'

Hubs can be set up by large employers trying to shift staff out of expensive head offices, or be run as businesses in their own right and open to all, making money from membership fees and in-house cafés. But they should also be a clear priority for local authorities who want to encourage residents to work nearer home: they're an obvious use for empty shops and pubs left vacant in the recession, perhaps even for libraries closed under spending cuts, and they have a key role in reducing commuting. When we spoke, Liz Wakeham-Jones was in talks with a Scottish local authority keen to use them to reduce traffic gridlock caused by workers travelling into the major city on their patch. But hubs could also ultimately contribute to a less easily defined social good, by rebuilding lives nearer home. 'I often hear anecdotally that flexible working is actually putting wealth back into local communities and encouraging better community relations,' says BT's Dennis Gissing. 'I used to commute from Suffolk and that used to take three and a half hours a day. There was no way I was going to be a school governor or manage the local football team.'

It's easy to sneer at the roots that people with time to spare put down in their communities, running Brownie packs and coaching children's football, but it's very short-sighted. Belonging to a local organisation makes us feel more trusting of others, more secure in our neighbourhood, happier with where we live.

People with strong social connections live longer, recover faster from illness and suffer less from depression and mental health problems than the socially isolated. Strong communities are ultimately cost-effective ones, which explains why politicians of all parties seem so suddenly nostalgic for a bygone age of neighbourliness.

When I bought my first London flat, I had the classic urban relationship with my neighbours, which is to say no relationship at all: when the little old lady next door moved into a nursing home I didn't notice the house was empty for well over a month. It was only later, on maternity leave with my son, that our little patch became anything more than a blur glimpsed from a late night taxi, or somewhere convenient to grab a coffee – or that I felt any glimmering of responsibility for it. Four years on, we live in a tight-knit village and I find myself baking cakes for the preschool fund-raiser and manning a stall at the village fete. Here you don't just know the neighbours, they wander in without knocking.

You can, of course, get this kind of social fix at the office; but what's lost is a certain richness of texture, since work friendships tend to be with people of similar age, class, educational background and skills, missing the quirks thrown up by simple proximity. Being able to work from, or near, home begins to answer some of the broader questions raised by family life too. It could free more of us to live nearer our extended families, helping us spread the load across the generations as described earlier in this book: being able to move across the country without giving up on satisfying, well-paid work is almost certainly part of the solution to the growing problem of caring for elderly parents, as well as for children.

But we are not yet seeing this big picture with sufficient clarity to act on it. The lesson from America is that real change in the working day happens when it's dramatically packaged, and when it's seen not as parents whining for special treatment but as pulling together for the greater good.

Just over two years ago, the US state of Utah launched an experimental four-day week for public sector workers – not as a sentimental gesture towards parents, but more brutally to cut office costs. Instead of working eight-hour days Monday to Friday, staff were moved on to compressed hours of ten hours a day for four days, with Fridays off. Over a year, the state of Utah saved $1.4 million on miles travelled in state-owned vehicles alone and three times that on reduced overtime and absenteeism. Carbon emissions and greenhouse gas emissions tumbled, as did petrol consumption.[4]

A compulsory four-day week doesn't suit parents keen to be at the school gate, nor perhaps non-parents keen to knock off early and enjoy their evenings. But by the end of the year, eight in ten Utah employees wanted the experiment to continue. And there are more consensual ways to draw together the threads of parenting, saving cash and saving the planet.

In Britain, the state does subsidise home working in a somewhat weedy way: you can claim a small percentage of domestic heating and lighting bills against tax. But that's no help to anyone whose employer is too suspicious of home working to let them try it. And while the junior transport minister Norman Baker last year began consulting on curbing commuting, in the first government paper I've seen to make the blindingly obvious connection between flexible working and reducing rush hour gridlock, that paper notes somewhat wanly that it's companies who bear the risk in working out how to do it and the rest of us who gain from fewer cars on the roads. What it failed to mention was that when government wants companies to do something for the good of the nation, the obvious tool to use is taxation.

Four years ago the state of Georgia launched a $20,000 tax

break for private companies willing to let some staff work at or near home, plus another credit of up to $1,200 for each new teleworker. Although the Telework Tax Credit was promoted as a way of reducing heavy pollution from commuting, it has obvious potential benefits for family life. Similarly, the Telework!VA project in Virginia offers a one-off payment of up to $50,000 in its most traffic-choked areas for employers prepared to let staff telework, under the slogan 'Don't Let Traffic Delay the Work Day'. Companies can claim for anything from home laptops to HR consultants, and the state doesn't just cover its costs, but actually profits: thanks to fewer miles being driven on their roads, and therefore lower maintenance and environmental costs, it estimates a $12 million return for taxpayers on the money spent.

In the UK, the 'green' gains from reducing commuting might be smaller, as Britons are already slightly more likely than Americans to commute by public transport instead of by car. But the reductions in greenhouse gas emissions caused by heating and lighting fewer offices could be considerable: BT calculates its staff reduce their carbon emissions by 14 per cent on average by starting to work from home. And I confess I'm more likely to turn off the lights and laptops when I've finished these days, now that they are pushing up my electricity bill and not the company's.

Besides, as the economy recovers we will share with Georgia and Virginia a very real fear of gridlock. According to research commissioned by the last government, on current trends about 13 per cent of traffic will be stuck in 'stop start travel conditions' – permanent traffic jams, creeping forward inch by fuming inch – by 2025. On trains, we can look forward to a 'substantial increase in already unacceptable overcrowding levels' by 2014.[5] There is talk of staggering the rush hour so that everybody isn't travelling at once – but it's work that needs staggering, since it's what causes the rush hour, and that will happen only when employers push for it as well as employees.

This summer offers an irresistible one-off opportunity to experiment with radical ideas for cutting commuter journeys, when the 2012 Olympic Games comes to London. Spectators for the Games are expected to create up to three million extra journeys a day at peak times. Anyone who has ever struggled to get on a packed Tube train can see why Transport for London warned last summer that work trips across the capital need to be cut by a third while the Games are on. Home working this July and August will arguably be not a perk but a necessity to keep the city (and its economy) from grinding to a halt. But once employers have bitten the bullet for the three weeks of the Olympics, why not encourage them to keep going?

The government's first step should be imposing a statutory duty on the public sector to encourage teleworking among staff wherever possible, modelled on similar federal regulations in America: it's madness to overlook potential savings in head office and energy costs where public money is at stake. But ministers should also consider the bolder step of tax reliefs for private employers prepared to let more staff work at or near home, modelled on those in Georgia and Virginia.

Another radical step would be a 'Free Friday' tax break for any employer able to negotiate with staff to shut the office completely one day a week, Utah-style – with staff either working from home, doing compressed hours with Friday off, or working part-time. Suddenly, the tables could be turned: a four-day week would now be in the boss's interests, not just in the staff's, and the underused 'full pay' options for flexibility would become commercially valuable at last. And while tax cuts unavoidably cost money, it's money this government is ideologically drawn towards spending: it believes tax cuts stimulate growth, which is why it is slashing corporation tax by 4 per cent over the period 2011–2015. What's more innately Conservative than a tax cut that stimulates business, reduces congestion and greenhouse gas emissions, boosts productivity and strengthens family life into the bargain by allowing families to have more time together? Time, as we have seen, is intimately linked to the survival of relationships as well as to the welfare of children.

The battle for time does, however, pose some serious challenges to the state, and to tax revenues in particular. In her 2010 book *Radical Homemakers*, charting the lives of Americans who have turned their back on working life as a protest against what they believe to be unsustainable capitalist lifestyles, Shannon Hayes tells the story of a mother who hired a Mexican nanny for her children so that she could go to work running a nanny agency, finding nannies for other mothers. This woman's own nanny, meanwhile, had left her children back in Mexico with relatives so that she could work overseas. The story is told as a striking example of what's wrong with a crazy world in which nobody is actually looking after their own children.

But that crazy world is, economically speaking, quite sane. The mother who runs the nanny agency earns a good wage, which she spends in the wider American economy; so do the women liberated to work by the nannies she finds for them, and to a lesser extent their nannies in turn. The poor Mexican nanny doubtless suffers most, but even she probably provides a lifestyle for her children back home that they wouldn't get without an American wage, and a valuable shot in the arm for her home country (remittances, or money sent home by migrant workers, to Mexico are that country's biggest earner after oil exports). To an economist, it makes perfect sense for these children to be apart from their parents: after all, a housewife pays no taxes, and creates no wealth.

It's only a short step from here to argue that being a wife, or even half of one, isn't just a private choice but a selfish public act: why aren't you out there not only working until you drop, but creating work for other people? The Danish economist Gøsta Esping-Andersen estimates that for every 100 women who go out to work, 15 new jobs are created from the outsourcing of the chores they no longer have time to do.[6] Families where both parents work hire cleaners and childminders, pay to get their groceries delivered, eat out to save cooking, run the car through the expensive jet wash.

The trouble with this argument is that many of the service jobs thus created are menial and badly paid, taken by poorer parents who are also now out of the home for long hours but can't afford to compensate by eating out at fancy restaurants. It's no fun being at the bottom of this pyramid of labour, and only fun at the top if you don't enjoy domesticity or feel no guilt about delegating it. It's a rather cold, bloodless vision of working life which grants no emotional and social value to time at home, and takes little account of either parents' or children's happiness. Not everything we value can, or should, be outsourced. But its greatest weakness is ignoring the inconvenient fact that some parents will simply give up work rather than give up on the family life they want.

It's true that by working fewer hours I have, arguably, cheated the public purse. For the first time in well over a decade I only just cleared the higher rate tax threshold in my first full year as a freelance – so that's a few thousand pounds the state used to get from me but doesn't now, which might have paid a nurse, or else some fraction of a missile fired at Libya. Private decisions have public consequences, tiny individually but profound en masse. Nine pounds of every ten collected in taxes actually come from the top 50 per cent of earners, which means that in the unlikely event of a three-day week becoming both routine for parents in senior jobs *and* a long-term lifestyle choice, the impact on the tax take (and on the public services those taxes support for the benefit of everyone else) could be severe. My time ultimately is someone else's money.

But a generation or two ago, middle-class mothers like me perhaps wouldn't have worked at all. It may simply be too greedy for governments to want both sexes to work at full stretch, instead of accepting that the price of swelling the workforce with hundreds of thousands more women may be that both sexes sometimes work a little less, but smarter, for a while – and that it's rising productivity, not rising hours, that will drive future growth. The fear of falling tax revenues is a reason not to panic and retreat but to get smarter: to make the changes outlined in this book that stop mothers abandoning decent jobs because they're overloaded at home and allow fathers to help without wrecking their own careers, and to create a flexible job market that lets both sexes sustain good careers after having children. Above all, it's a reason to encourage the 'full pay' options for parents which don't involve paying a penny less in tax, precisely by experimenting with options like a four-day office week. But the current UK government seems strangely lacking in a confident, coherent story to tell about families which might lead it towards an integrated half a wife model. We can't tell whether it takes a stern economist's view of family life, in which everyone who can work should do so, or more of a sympathetic fellow parent's.

On the one hand, offering a married tax allowance purely to couples where one doesn't work suggests a strong nostalgia for the dying days of sole breadwinners. On the other, proposals for sharing maternity leave between couples are a thumping vote of confidence in dual career parenting. (And this muddle isn't just the result of coalition: the Conservative minister Theresa May was pushing the idea of shared leave long before she wound up sharing power with the more progressive Liberal Democrats.) The Chancellor is accused of trying to force women back to the kitchen sink, with cuts to childcare subsidy; the welfare secretary thinks more single mothers on benefits should go out to work. The most generous interpretation of this muddle is that the government doesn't much care what families do, so long as it works – but I doubt that's how most Conservative MPs (or indeed Conservative voters) would see it. The only thing that is crystal clear is the government's strong desire for more couples to stay together, and raise their children together, for life.

It's not a bad place to start: the desire for happier, more stable relationships between parents is an important thread running through this book because it's what most of us start out wanting too. Few people embark on a love affair, still less a planned and wanted pregnancy, hoping it will all go wrong. But while it's true, as Conservatives never tire of saying, that married parents are statistically less likely to split up than cohabiting parents, to assume that the answer lies in making everyone get (and stay) married is confusing cause with effect. It's not the wedding itself, but the self-selecting nature of those who still choose to wed, now that being unmarried parents is no longer shocking, that counts. (For example, those with a strong religious belief in lifelong commitment are more likely to get married, but it's the belief rather than the big white frock and the confetti that keeps them together: putting a very different couple through the same ceremony might not bring the same result.) Wedding rings have no magical properties in themselves, as plenty of happily committed cohabiting parents could testify – and one good parent certainly beats two inadequate, neglectful or violent ones.

And even if marriage was the magic bullet, it's unlikely that the princely offer of a £3 a week tax break (but only if one of you gives up work) would be enough to put divorce lawyers out of business. There are far better ways to spend £550 million on keeping parents together.

For less than 5 per cent of that amount, you could double Relate's budget to counsel couples on the brink of separation, married or not. Sometimes counselling is enough to save a relationship: but if not, it can allow couples to vent their anger in a more constructive way than arguing over who gets the children for half-term, and so to part on more civilised terms. For those whose relationships genuinely can't be saved, the goal must be ensuring that the end of marriage doesn't mean the end of joint parenthood.

I don't think the answer lies in changing the law to grant fathers an automatic presumption of shared care, as the angrily vocal divorced fathers' lobby wants: it's the child's happiness, not their parents' demands, that should take precedence. But the American concept of collaborative law is worth exploring.

It's still a relatively rare way of conducting British divorces, but under collaborative law couples agree from the start not to go to court. Instead of rival lawyers thrashing their claims out before a judge, financial and custody settlements are decided in private 'four-way meetings' where both partners and their lawyers meet face to face. It may not suit families with highly complex finances, or those just too angry to be in the same room; but it can be kinder and quicker (and cheaper) than a conventional legal battle. We should be training more divorce lawyers in collaborative techniques – and since one in three children are now raised by unmarried parents who are outside formal divorce law, we should be making a collaborative-style separation process available to them too.

Last but not least, given the evidence that sharing the 'wife work' could help lower the risk of divorce, a government genuinely interested in avoiding the trauma and expense of family breakdown should be seriously considering how to help couples help each other. If money can buy one thing for working parents, it's time.

Taking back the one or two days a week recommended in this book may seem an impossible luxury for lower earners. Men in particular will often rule out working less if it means earning less, and as more women become breadwinners they are beginning to experience the same pressures. Children are undeniably expensive, with the bulk of the cost unhelpfully front-loaded: the biggest chunk of the estimated £210,000 it costs to raise a child to the age of 18 is the £67,430 for childcare,[7] which is disproportionately expensive in the first five years. Parents of teenagers may look back nostalgically to the days when their offspring were happy playing with a cardboard box, but they're forgetting the hidden costs of having preschoolers, either in childcare or in salary sacrificed to be at home. The cost of parenting is concentrated just when parents would most like to be working less.

We need to smooth out these costs over the decades, using the times of relative feast in a lifetime's earnings – before children come along, and again as children grow up, when adults are free to work longer hours – to subsidise the times of famine.

There used to be a good excuse for not saving up before having children: in generations past, the period between starting work and having children was short and relatively badly paid. But for the 'concertina generation', the golden advantage of that punishing combination of early success and late childbirth is the extra time to save for what lies ahead. When I look back at the money I blew on vodka and black cabs in my twenties, I could weep for the choices it might give me now.

Saving for a family rarely occurs to recent graduates because all that seems so far in the distance: impossible to imagine being as old as 30. But despite our regularly bemoaned lack of savings culture, over half of Britons aged between 30 and 50 *are* actually saving enough for a comfortable retirement.[8] We save when it's easy, enrolling in a company pension scheme if you can just tick a box to join; when it's affordable, since the biggest reason given for not saving is having no money to spare; and when given the right emotional nudge.

The biggest reason for anyone to save is that money liberates. Having something stashed away enables you to walk out on a bad relationship, a bad job, a bad neighbourhood: money means being able to reject the choices others would make for you. And that, I eventually realised, was why long before I had my own son I started a bank account for my newborn niece. I put money aside for Martha so that she wouldn't be powerless, as too many women are, to change something when she needed to. Money means choices and freedom, rather than feeling economically unable to provide the time you think your child needs.

What I'd like to see is the personal finance equivalent of a wedding trousseau, the 'bottom drawer' in which young women used to put things away for a future married life: a place for young people of both sexes who would like a family one day to start saving for it, in a long-term savings vehicle with attractive interest rates and a long notice period (nine months seems appropriate). It could be marketed at those in their first jobs, and since not too many 20-year-old men are drawn to wedding trousseaux, it would have to be branded with its ultimate purpose – freedom to live your life as you see fit. It's not that, in high streets crowded with banks, we lack ways to save. What we lack is powerful enough reminders at key stages of our lives that – old-fashioned as it sounds – it helps to plan for a family. What we need is a Life Bank.

A generous government could make Life Bank savings tax-free

for lower earners, to help them afford more time with their families: but the accounts could be set up at minimal state cost initially, administered by the personal finance industry. Employers could chip into staff's Life Banks as a perk of the job, rather like free medical insurance, perhaps linking these payments to length of service. Parents could chip in towards future grandchildren (or fond aunts towards their nieces). Life Banks could be promoted by the wedding industry, and while I don't personally favour state subsidy for marriage, a traditionally minded government might make a small one-off deposit to the Life Bank for a couple on their wedding or civil partnership day. (Guests might also find it a longer-lived gift than wine glasses.)

Savings could be withdrawn after the first six weeks of maternity leave – when the state stops paying 90 per cent of the mother's salary – and although it would be prohibitively nosy for banks to ask what families were doing with it, the account should be marketed as offering couples more choice in rearranging their working lives, covering anything from subsidising reduced hours to starting a business. For those who start out hoping for children but for whatever reason don't manage it, Life Bank savings could be rolled over into pensions or drawn down after 55, to subsidise a change of career then.

It might seem strangely self-defeating for governments or employers to invest in anything that helps people to work less. But it happens more often than you'd think. Bosses offer more generously paid maternity leave than the legal minimum because they know it helps attract and keep staff; politicians doubled maternity leave to a year partly in the hope that a gentler, slower re-entry to working life would mean fewer parents panicking and giving up work altogether. Several countries already offer their citizens ways of locking up money for the long term but raiding it to help with major life events: the American retirement plan known as the 401(k) allows for withdrawals in a personal crisis such as major illness, while the Netherlands has its Life Course Savings Scheme, enabling families to save up for parental leave. However, as the history of savings plans suggests Life Banks would almost certainly appeal more to middle-class parents than to struggling lower earners with no cash to spare, what's really needed is a rethink of the way the welfare state tracks parents' lives.

From next year, it's currently proposed that child benefit should be withdrawn from the UK's higher rate taxpayers, turning it overnight into a payment mainly for these struggling 'squeezed middle' families. This is the perfect opportunity for reform so that it better meets their needs. Child benefit is currently paid at a flat rate throughout the child's life (just over £82 a month for a first child in 2011), which means it's enough to cover the milk and nappy bill in the baby years, but nowhere near enough to subsidise parents who want to work less. Yet surprisingly, according to the welfare minister Frank Field, over a child's lifetime from birth to 19 a parent can receive up to £100,000 in child benefit and tax credits combined (of which just under a quarter is likely to be child benefit). We're not using that money nearly smartly enough.

Asked by the government in 2010 to produce a review on boosting children's life chances, Field initially flirted with reforming child benefit so that parents got lump sums of up to £25,000 in the first three years of a child's life and only a trickle of cash thereafter. The idea sank without trace, possibly because it would have been eye-wateringly expensive, with huge upfront costs for newborn babies, while the savings from cutting benefits as they grew up would not be fully recovered for 19 years. Since £25,000 is more than an average year's salary, it would also encourage parents not to work at all – making it harder for them to pick up their careers again when the benefits abruptly ran out.

Yet Field was right that spending isn't matching the way we live. We should be gradually increasing child benefit for under-fives, and gradually fading it out for children over the age of 11, aiming towards a goal of £3,500 a year per child in the preschool years – roughly the amount of salary lost, after tax, by a parent on average earnings doing a four-day instead of a five-day week. It wouldn't cover the cost of half a wife, but it would help: and while parents of older teenagers would receive less than they do at present, they should have greater freedom than parents of toddlers to work and earn.

But there is one last place the government could sensibly put some money, and it is not into the pockets of parents. Two years ago, I was coming out of the library on a sunny spring day with my son when a well-dressed woman about my age stopped us on the street. She apologised for bothering us but said she was trying to find part-time childcare for her five-year-old daughter. She worked at a local hospital, which meant late shifts, but couldn't find a nursery or childminder open past 6 p.m. If she couldn't find something she would have to stop work, and having unsuccessfully asked everyone she knew she was now desperate enough to stop complete strangers like me on the street in the hope of finding a mother with whom to work out an informal arrangement. And all this was in the middle of the so-called 'Mumsnet election' of 2010, during which politicians were falling over each other to woo middle-class mothers. Every day brought some photo opportunity involving fingerpaints – yet nobody was discussing problems like this. I often wonder, uncomfortably, what happened to that mother and that little girl.

We live in a 24/7 economy, with supermarkets and call centres open round the clock: the public sector relies heavily on people working sometimes highly variable shifts set at only a few weeks' notice. We have an army of self-employed workers not sure exactly what they've got on from one week to the next, and of part-timers who occasionally want to swap their days around in a crisis. But childcare is still overwhelmingly organised to suit a fixed 9–5 working day, Monday to Friday, with sessions fixed and booked terms in advance, when for millions of people work is no longer like this. For such parents, the problem isn't just money, it's that there is no suitable childcare to spend it on. And ultimately that poses a problem for business too.

Back in the 1990s, some of the loudest and most persuasive lobbying for more state-subsidised childcare – to which first John Major and then Tony Blair responded – actually came not from parents but from employers. People won't work if childcare costs more than they earn. They'll either stay at home or demand much higher wages, neither of which helps profits, and so big business realised that for the state to spend more on childcare would take the pressure off them. If they allow government to backslide on childcare now, employers will once again be the losers.

Neither my own full-time job nor my freelance career would have been possible without flexible childcare – first a great nanny, and then a great childminder, without whom the whole tottering house of cards would have collapsed. But nannies are expensive, and flexible childminders are a threatened species because they can't swap sessions at short notice unless they keep some of their spaces empty, which isn't profitable. Local authorities used to pay childminders and preschools extra for being flexible, via a top-up to the funding for three- and four-year-olds' free places, but these grants are now being wiped out by spending cuts. It's a false economy that should be reversed.

Nurseries do need to know how many children are coming and when, because they are legally required to maintain a set ratio of staff to children. But a series of experiments with 'pay as you go' childcare run by the national charity 4Children, of which I'm a trustee, suggests even this problem is not insuperable. In several of its nurseries parents can book as little as an hour at a time, or blocks of a few hours, at short notice: there is usually a settled 'core' of children doing the same sessions every week, but the rest vary as their parents – who tend to be young, and often studying rather than working – need. It means a hectic juggling act for the nursery manager, but it works.

The trouble is once again that it's not as profitable, because if fewer parents than expected turn up then the nursery will be overstaffed. As Charles Ellis, deputy executive of 4Children points out, 'We're happy if we make a surplus: we see we are meeting a social objective. But why would a private company do that?' Nonetheless, the model now exists for filling even this difficult gap in the childcare market. And if someone – either local employers needing a very flexible workforce, or perhaps the state – is prepared to subsidise them, a whole range of providers could potentially fill it.

Perhaps surprisingly, however, the biggest area of unmet demand for childcare in survey after survey isn't for these rather 'niche' hours. It's for the one thing every single working parent has to deal with sooner or later: school holidays. When my son was small, I used hazily to imagine the onset of primary school as a kind of bittersweet parole date, when working mothers might be freed from the weight of daytime guilt and stay-at-home mothers make free with all that intoxicating liberty. It was only in the spring my son turned four that I realised life isn't like that.

School presents both a frustratingly small and a dauntingly big problem for working parents. The small problem is the gap between a 9 a.m. to 3 p.m. school day and an 8 a.m. to 6 p.m. working one – often too few hours to interest a childminder or a nanny, but too many to wing it. The big problem is the yawning expanse of summer, in which adult annual leave makes only a modest dent. How did a child's day, and year, get so out of kilter with a parent's?

Right now, we are fudging this question. A third of parents use breakfast and after-school clubs, meaning their children are on school premises potentially from 8 a.m. to 6 p.m.: not strictly speaking in class, but not exactly letting off steam in chess club either. Such 'wraparound' school provision is a lifesaver for parents, especially lone ones, but anyone who has ever tried to reason with an exhausted five-year-old at the end of a day like this can find themselves guiltily wondering whose good it's for.

This is a sensitive issue, in which private unease conflicts with public principles. One leading expert on working parenthood told me her own organisation is not publicly against extended schools, but personally she has strong reservations: 'Children have very different body clocks and levels of energy and attention spans. By 3.30 p.m. an eight-year-old needs to go home, frankly: it doesn't need another two hours of stimulation. I know too many of my children's friends who are just basically unhappy with after-school clubs. There is a problem but it is not the child's problem, it is ours as adults.'[9] My own feeling is that while it's entirely understandable for parents to use after-school clubs and some young children obviously do enjoy them, they aren't for everyone; the child who finds school tiring or difficult, let alone the one who's bullied, sometimes just needs the sanctuary of home. And that's where the creation of the much more open market in flexible jobs discussed in the last chapter becomes critical.

Home working, in a job where you can shuffle work around and into the evenings if necessary, or flexitime can help enormously (as of course can a good childminder, who will take children after school during term times and full time in the holidays, or for older children an au pair). But the benefit of the half a wife model is that if parents can cover two days of the school week between them, the remaining three days may start to feel more manageable. If a grandparent, older relative or good friend with whom you can swap childcare favours can take on one day, then a couple of long days a week in after-school club may not feel too bad. The big question is how old a child needs to be before they can manage something like a full 'adult' working week.

We are, in fact, already seeing the creeping introduction of a 9-to-5 day for secondary school children by stealth, with surprisingly little debate over whether it's what parents (or children) actually want. When Tony Blair set up the first wave of academy schools to replace failing inner city schools, they were given not only spanking new buildings as a sign of rebirth but a range of unique freedoms, including the power to vary opening hours. Several academies promptly introduced a 9-to-5 teaching day (often opening at 7.30 for breakfast). Since then, they've been joined by the coalition government's planned 'free schools' set up outside local authority control, which have powers to vary both hours and term dates.

Academies have variously used the extra time to let pupils do homework, change lesson structures so that less time is wasted traipsing between classrooms, or to let teachers set and mark more work during the day. But they have also freed parents to do something like a normal working day, without worrying about where their children are. More than one in ten schools in England and Wales are already academies, with all schools now eligible to apply, so before long a significant proportion of children may be doing a 9-to-5 day: yet there has been very little discussion of the implications.

Logically, more teaching should mean children learning more, but that isn't always the case. The first wave of academies were dealing with struggling pupils, often from chaotic backgrounds, who benefited from all the teaching they could get; but a longer day wouldn't necessarily benefit all children in the same way. Some parents will undoubtedly resent seeing less of their children, and some who already feel their children are over-tested in school will worry about piling on more pressure. There are no easy answers and the needs of big-city parents may be different from those in small rural schools, but it's time politicians began a public debate about precisely what parents want from schools, including whether all schools should be free to vary their hours – subject, perhaps, to balloting parents and consulting schools nearby – or shorten the long summer holidays.

While we fondly imagine the holidays are designed around children's need to run wild, in reality they have always revolved around the demands of adult work: they are a hangover from a lost agricultural Britain, where children helped with the harvest in summer. For poorer children in particular, there is now good evidence that six weeks off in summer is damaging – they fall back, forget things, and spend much of September relearning what they knew in July (although middle-class children seem to regress less). At least one of Michael Gove's new 'free schools', the Norwich Free School in Norfolk, takes just a month off in summer (and even during holidays offers wraparound childcare from 8.15 a.m. to 5.45 p.m. for all but one week of the year). As a leaked Downing Street memo confirmed last September, there is strong interest within government in a shorter summer holiday but some nervousness over how to proceed.

Longer days and shorter holidays are expensive, since teachers' wages are the biggest cost a school has. But there are ways around it, according to a report produced last year by the Teach First scheme, which fast-tracks bright graduates into schools as teachers for a short period. It cited a New York school that increased pupils' time in class without making staff work more hours via a radical job redesign. Some teachers started earlier or finished later than usual, heads did more teaching, and instead of having set school holidays the teachers had bookable holidays throughout the year. Hiring more teachers and rotating holidays might allow more imaginative rostering over longer terms.

Any change to the school day would also require balancing the needs of parents and children very carefully against the rights of teachers as employees. Teachers do cherish the long summer breaks to recuperate from what is an emotionally intense job, and for teachers who are parents themselves the ability to spend this time with their own children is invaluable. But does that make them intrinsically different from, say, nurses or police officers, whose jobs are also intense, and who also miss their children? Is it right that parents' working lives are dictated by the outcome of sporadic skirmishes between teaching unions and ministers, who tend to fiddle occasionally at the fringes of this argument before retreating? We elect politicians at least partly to exercise the judgement of Solomon on sensitive issues, after all.

There is a bigger question than school timetabling which successive governments have so far nervously ducked, however. There is one last step politicians could take which would represent a quantum leap forward for the half a wife model, but it's one that is puzzlingly seldom discussed. It concerns the status of fathers in the eyes of the law.

Given what we know about how men and women influence each other's working lives, it should be clear by now that real change in family life will be at best grindingly slow to come unless fathers are genuinely free to make different choices. And frankly, that is unlikely to happen while fathers remain vulnerable to a backlash at work from which mothers are, however inadequately and patchily at times, protected.

Mothers earn less over their lifetime than childfree women not just because they tend to work shorter hours, or avoid certain careers; sometimes it is really about the boss's revenge, a vindictive decision to deny a woman promotion or ensure she's first in line for redundancy just for having dared to give birth. At least when that happens, working mothers can fall back on some basic protection under the law. But for working fathers, things can be very different.

A mother treated in this way will often sue for sex discrimination. As Sarah Jackson, of Working Families, points out, only around one per cent of cases where a request for flexible working is rejected end up being challenged at tribunal: but that's because most women just sue for sex discrimination, which offers wider grounds for challenge than the law governing flexible working. Even if she doesn't have a male colleague to compare herself against, a woman can sue by claiming indirect discrimination – basically, arguing that because women are more likely than men to have childcare responsibilities, punishing staff for having children is particularly unfair to women. But a father victimised in the same way can find himself, quite literally, in no man's land.

The case of Neil Walkingshaw, a mechanic from East Lothian who sued his employers when they wouldn't let him go part-time to look after his baby son, established over a decade ago that men can claim sex discrimination if they're not allowed to reduce their hours when female colleagues are. But if a firm treats mothers just as badly as fathers, or if a man works in a male-dominated world without any mothers to compare himself against, then he's in trouble. Men can't claim for indirect sex discrimination, since the law still assumes it's largely women who look after children, and women whose careers sometimes suffer for it. And that leaves a big hidden hole in the safety net.

Among the callers to Working Families' legal helpline two years ago was a father of three young children, whose wife had left him. For his job he had to travel overnight about once a month, but he couldn't do so any more because of having to look after the children, which annoyed his boss even though he was still hitting his sales targets. This father could have formally requested flexible working, but if it was rejected by this unsympathetic boss he would have been stuck: there were no mothers in his office against whom to compare himself, so he couldn't sue for sex discrimination. Yet if the situations were reversed and this man had left his wife in the lurch with the children, she would have enjoyed the full support of the law in bargaining with her boss, backed up by the threat of suing for indirect discrimination. It can't be fair that two people suffering from an identical problem are treated differently just because one is a mother and one is a father; and it can't be entirely surprising, either, that some fathers won't risk trying to work differently when the law won't support them.

The law as it stands can be seen as unfair on women too. If a childless woman wouldn't have been made redundant or refused a bonus, why should a mother have to go through the farce of pretending it's all about gender when it's really about giving birth? It perpetuates the idea of women as fragile victims, and it fails to name and confront the real problem.

The occasional dinosaur will still refuse to hire a woman simply because she's a woman, and until they are extinct the legal requirement not to discriminate on grounds of sex should remain. But young women are increasingly experiencing an equal playing field in study and at work, at least until they have children: the biggest professional hurdle they now face is not gender, but motherhood. Childfree women face their own battles, with whispering campaigns about why they haven't had a family or unfair assumptions about how 'hard' they must be, but their progression to the top is probably smoother: it's estimated that half of women in higher level and management occupations in Britain don't have children.[10]

There is a way out of this tangled mess, and it is simply to call a spade a spade. If the real problem isn't gender but parenthood, for both sexes, then that is what we should be publicly debating. It's irrational discrimination against people on the grounds of family status that should be outlawed.

The very idea will no doubt horrify the business lobby; although most people accept now that you shouldn't refuse to hire a woman purely because she's a woman, many employers do believe it's logical to treat childless employees differently from parents. You may encourage a senior woman going on maternity leave to come back, but should the childless woman who works overtime while she's away really not get rewarded for her efforts? Can't the single man willing to move to the New York office at a month's notice be promoted over his rival, who won't go anywhere because his children are settled at British schools? Might there even be furious legal challenges from the childfree, wanting to know why their status as non-parents isn't equally respected and they never get holidays in August?

In fact, something like a family-related discrimination law already operates surprisingly close to home. State employers in Northern Ireland are already legally obliged to treat staff with dependants the same as staff without: the idea is you shouldn't lose out because you have a child to look after, regardless of gender. South of the border, it gets more radical: in the Republic of Ireland, discrimination at work on the grounds of 'family status' was banned over a decade ago, protecting not just parents but anyone who lives with and cares for a seriously disabled person. It has its roots in a commitment in the Irish constitution to 'protect the family', derived from the importance placed on marriage and children by the Catholic faith.

Similarly in America, a serious debate has begun over so-called 'family-related discrimination' at work. There's no federal law against it yet, but it's banned outright in Alaska, and in New Jersey public sector employees can't be discriminated against on grounds of 'familial status'. Best practice guidance recently issued by the official US equal opportunities watchdog advised that employers should neither make assumptions about mothers' commitment nor assume that male workers 'do not, or should not, have significant caregiving responsibilities' – and significantly, that they shouldn't treat childless women more favourably than mothers.[11] America is slowly recognising the elephant in the room: not gender, but children.

It should be possible to draft a creatively worded British family discrimination law which recognises that parenting is neither unique to women nor an unpardonable sin, but still lets employers make reasonable exceptions. Our existing sex discrimination law is hedged nervously around with get-out clauses, after all, still allowing for female patients who only want to see a female GP or for the preservation of gentlemen's clubs. A review of discrimination law could also examine whether moving towards outlawing discrimination on grounds of family status might mean some specific regulations covering mothers could be scrapped. It's not about bolting fathers on to the existing law, but redesigning it to acknowledge that 'parent' doesn't necessarily equal mother and that parenthood, not gender, is sometimes the problem.

Employers should understand, too, that the alternative is change sneaking in via the back door without public debate over its limits or safeguards. Five years ago, I interviewed a rather nervous but determined legal secretary called Sharon Coleman for *The Observer*: she was suing her employer after being put at risk of redundancy, claiming that she was victimised because her four-year-old son Oliver had been seriously ill since birth and she needed time off to care for him. Shortly after we met, she won a landmark victory under disability discrimination law, after arguing that despite being able-bodied herself she had suffered discrimination by association with her disabled son. That judgment was the first step for millions of carers, whether they look after sick children or parents or spouses, towards a right to equal treatment with non-carers – a right they had not been given by any elected politician. The first piece of the legal jigsaw is already in place. And the second may well come from pioneer fathers realising just how puny their employment rights are, compared to their wives'.

Men will have the right to get their old jobs back after taking the proposed new split parental leave, so they can't be fired for taking time out. But it's less clear what happens if they are then subtly sidelined, or undermined, or denied the juicy new client because nobody can be sure they won't have another baby next year; if, in other words, they are treated like mothers. Will there be a 'daddy penalty' for taking time out, as there has long been for mothers, in terms of pay? Will the careers of men with and without children start to diverge?

So far, too, it's only mothers who will get 90 per cent of salary for the first few weeks of split parental leave, while men will receive the pittance that is statutory maternity pay. Personally, I think that time to recover physically from the birth is essentially a form of sick leave and should be paid differently from 'optional' time with the baby, but some big City firms are already quietly discussing paying fathers who take the leave the same rates as mothers to prevent any legal unpleasantness. Would employers really prefer these issues to be settled higgledy-piggledy through the courts, by unelected judges hearing test cases, or thrashed out openly in parliament where all sides can influence the debate? These are profound changes in our national way of life, and should be treated as such.

It can seem hard to justify so much upheaval just to solve the everyday dilemmas of our domestic lives – even when they affect, as we have seen, one in four voters and over 12 million people. But politicians dwell with such hideous sentimentality on the idea of family life for a reason. The family is where so much public policy starts and ends, and it's good parenting that often determines its failure or success. It is impossible to raise school standards without remembering that parents are a child's first and most influential teachers: impossible to tackle crime effectively without recognising that offending behaviour is often rooted in childhood misery, unless you think it's just coincidence that prisoners are 13 times more likely than the average person to have been in care. It makes no sense to try and improve public health without recognising that how much television a five-year-old watches, slumped motionless on the sofa, can predict their chances of being overweight at 30. And it is completely impossible to construct an economic policy without acknowledging both that working patterns change post-parenthood and that families are a critical economic unit, the tiny cells whose health influences that of a much bigger organism. There's a reason why the word 'economy' derives from the Greek for 'household management'.

What looks like a private dilemma between a parent and child can spread very quickly first to the marriage, then through the extended family. It can draw in two sets of employers, spill out into wider society, and finally touch the state itself. Arguments that begin over the kitchen table do sometimes lead to the Cabinet table, and all I have tried to do here is trace that process, to show the interconnectedness of things: to see how work interacts with a marriage as well as with children, how men and women can either shrink or expand each other's choices, how employers' interests can converge happily with those of parents or the state (and why they don't, when they don't). It may feel daunting to see how small a cog each parent is in such a big and complicated machine. But it shouldn't make us feel helpless: quite the opposite.

Back in 1994, the astronomer Carl Sagan showed a slide at a public lecture featuring a tiny blue dot suspended between two white slashes of light. It was, he explained, an image of Earth taken from four billion miles away by the space probe Voyager, and unlike the familiar image of the Earth as seen from space – that startlingly beautiful blue and green globe, hanging in the darkness – it captures our utter insignificance. We are, he told his students, just 'a lonely speck in the great enveloping cosmic dark': every war ever fought, every drop of blood shed, the sum total of all human civilisation adds up to one dust mote in the sky. But, Sagan continued, to him this knowledge merely underlined our responsibility not just to deal more compassionately with each other but 'to preserve and cherish that pale blue dot, the only home we've ever known'. This is the only life you'll ever know. Take it back.

EPILOGUE

More than two decades ago now, in the fog between school and university, I spent a long hot dizzy summer studying Italian in Florence. And it was there that I learned, among quite other things, the art of getting lost on purpose: or how to get under the skin of a foreign city by wandering deliberately away from what is known. In a small city like Florence, the deliberately lost will sooner or later always find their way back home, having in all likelihood stumbled across something new – a hidden piazza, a bar they'll never quite be able to find again – in the space of an ostensibly wasted afternoon.

As the novelist Audrey Niffenegger puts it in *Her Fearful Symmetry*, a tale of American twins adrift in London, there are two ways to treat getting lost: one is to panic, and the other 'to abandon yourself to lostness, to allow the fact that you've misplaced yourself to change the way you experience the world'. It now seems to me that what I did nearly two years ago was to get myself lost on purpose. I misplaced myself, in the hope of changing something.

Fairy tales and myths are full of dire warnings about what happens to those who wander from the proper path, some of which I now read to my son. He was fascinated for a while by Hansel and Gretel, abandoned in the woods, unable to follow their carefully scattered breadcrumbs home; I am more taken lately by Dorothy in *The Wizard of Oz*, straying from the Yellow Brick Road into the prettily beguiling poppy field and falling into a drugged slumber. What I have learned from many of the people I spoke to for this book is that it does not do to linger too long among the poppies. Slip too far into maternal unconsciousness, and you might not wake up again.

But there isn't much to be said for sticking grimly to the Yellow Brick Road, either: the shimmering green city to which it led contained only an illusion of power and privilege, and a most ungrateful wizard. Fortune favours the bold, at least in storybooks. How did it work out for me?

At the end of my first year off the beaten track, I sat down to do the reckoning. I earned roughly half my old newspaper salary, but then I probably halved my hours; and since the hidden costs of my working plummeted once I didn't need a full-time nanny or a ruinous London mortgage, even my dubious maths suggest that financially it has worked out fine so far.

There have undeniably been things I have missed, particularly a certain kind of London life that I no longer lead, although in reality I led it far less often anyway after having a baby. And I never walk past the Houses of Parliament without feeling a certain fleeting kind of sadness. But I have done things professionally that I simply wouldn't have been able to do without leaving: work is broader, richer and more interesting than it would have been had I stayed in the gilded cage.

Life at home, meanwhile, has turned out both immeasurably better and sometimes worse than I thought it might. In my old daydreams, giving up the job was supposed to mean finally having time for all the things I felt bad about not doing with my son, like trips to the zoo and intricately creative ways with potato printing. And in my new spare time I'd learn to ice-skate, finally get curtains made for the bathroom, stick all the photographs in the album instead of shoving them in a box in the loft . . .

The reality, now I am home more often, is of course nothing like my fond imaginings. Domestic life is not perfect: the house plants are still half dead, the photograph albums still half empty. But I am less bothered by trivial imperfections, and more honest with myself about why I don't do some of the things I thought I was too busy for. The reason I don't go running every day, it turns out, is not lack of time but a deep lack of enthusiasm.

The unexpected twist has been the way my confidence as a mother was shaken, at first, by actually doing more mothering. No longer the absent mummy sweeping grandly in at bedtime to be greeted with rapture, I have had both to get used to being taken for granted, and to face up to my own shortcomings. A few short months with a toddler and no childcare, cramming work into the gaps when he slept, blew a hole in any lingering delusions about having the temperament for full-time motherhood.

But there is a relief in learning to know one's limits like this. Being here more has freed me to worry less about being a fairy-tale 'good mother' – one armed with endless bright ideas for making jigsaws from scratch – and more about being my son's idea of a good mother, namely someone prepared to let him dig up the flowerbeds looking for bugs. Small children are naturally good at the art of living slow, until hustled out of it by their frantic parents; and so I have learned to listen more, rush less, and spread out experiences so that we can actually enjoy them rather than always trying to cram in more. Living this kind of life only became possible when I stopped feeling the terrible itch to overcompensate for my absence. And in turn, on the three days I currently work, I don't feel guilty about doing it at full throttle.

But a year and a half in, this still feels like only the start of a process. Every tectonic shift triggers a string of little aftershocks, and I'm told it takes anywhere up to three years for the chain reaction within a family to fizzle out. Had I not been living a different life alongside him, and forcing him to listen to endless half-baked theories for this book, I doubt my husband would ever have given so much thought to his own working life – nor so much more time to our life as a family.

The ultimate test of our resolve came just as I was finishing the book. After taking a few months out while I was writing it, my husband was offered a terrific but demanding job: ironically, a few weeks after he accepted, it was my turn to get a rather intriguing offer out of the blue. For one brief afternoon, we pondered going back to a life where we were both absorbed in work around the clock. It didn't take very long to decide that there was no going back.

Besides, a new life lies ahead for all of us soon. My son is nearly ready to start school, and I am intensely aware of the loss of something: the symbiotic intimacy of the baby years is already gone, and he will never be quite such a part of me again. It is the beginning of a very long, slow process of letting go, and perhaps the possibility of grasping hold of something else. It's hard to imagine that would ever be a conventional office job again, but lately I have found myself scribbling spidery flow charts on the back of shopping lists, tentative maps of new projects I might try. Perhaps it's time to get a little lost again: but at least these days, I know the way back home.

ACKNOWLEDGEMENTS

This book would never have seen the light of day had it not been for a group of people I sadly can't name: the parents who agreed to tell me, with remarkable and often moving candour, about their own working and family life. They all did so on the promise of anonymity, but they know who they are, and I only hope they feel I did their stories justice.

I also need to thank my own circle of 'mummy friends', with whom I have laughed until I cried over the years (and occasionally cried until I laughed), and without whom I would never have got through the nappy years with sufficient sanity to write this book. The nicest thing that nobody ever tells you about parenthood is the depth of the camaraderie that exists between its survivors. And nothing I've achieved as a working mother would have been possible without two people I count myself incredibly lucky to have known: first our son's nanny, Lili James, and subsequently his childminder, Tracey Harris.

For the purposes of this book, I've picked an awful lot of brains, but among those who aren't directly quoted in its pages I should thank Katherine Rake of the national Family and Parenting Institute and Kitty Ussher, ex-director of Demos, for their time; and Nicola Jeal, now of *The Times*, and *The Observer*'s John Mulholland for suggesting I write the original article that eventually and somewhat indirectly led to this book.

Nor would it have taken quite the shape it did without Yvette Cooper, MP, then Secretary of State for Work and Pensions, persuading me after I resigned to join a government task force on encouraging flexible working. After years of hanging around Westminster I thought I knew how decisions were taken (and why sometimes they weren't): seeing it from the inside made me realise I didn't know the half of it. The experience was hugely helpful in understanding how to make change happen.

Talking of making changes happen, I am immensely grateful to my editor at Chatto & Windus, Becky Hardie. I wanted to work with her as soon as I met her, because I knew she would push me harder than most: what I didn't know was that she would do it with such charm and good humour. I also owe a large debt to Karolina Sutton at Curtis Brown, for knocking my ideas into shape and being a fount of fascinating publishing gossip, and to Peter Beaumont for introducing me to her. Meanwhile without the confidence shown in me at various stages and in various ways by John Foscolo, Peter Moore, Ian MacGregor, David Hughes and Roger Alton, I wouldn't have had a career in political journalism worth giving up in the first place.

But in the true spirit of half a wife, this project has inevitably been a family affair. I'm eternally grateful to my sister Sophie and brother-in-law Ian (not to mention Martha, Jude and Reuben) for rescuing me from more than one childcare crisis during the final, crazed edits; but it's my husband James who has played an awful lot of zoo games while I've been off muttering to myself in the study. He has lived uncomplainingly with this book for over a year, and I couldn't have done it without him.

Lastly, I want to thank my parents, Geoff and Judy, for all their love and support over the years – and for teaching me everything I really need to know about family life.

NOTES

PROLOGUE

1   Data from European Labour Force Survey, in 'The World's Women 2000: Trends and Statistics', report published by the United Nations, 2000.

2   Office of National Statistics, Labour Market Statistics, 31 March 2011.

3   *Families and Work*, Office of National Statistics, July 2005.

4   'Time Use & Childcare', Equal Opportunities Commission, 2003.

5   Census, 2001.

6   *Third Work Life Balance Employee Survey*, Department of Trade & Industry, March 2007.

7   IPSOS-Mori International Women's Day poll for EQUALS, February 2011.

8   *The Feminine Mystique*, Betty Friedan, 1963.

9   Interview in *The Guardian*, 2 October 2010.

1. THE LURE OF HOME

1 Association of Chartered Certified Accountants Survey, September 2009.

2 British Social Attitudes Survey, 2009.

3 Corporate Executive Board Quarterly, *Employee Engagement Trends*, 2009.

4 Wayne Hochwarter, Tyler Everett and Stuart Tapley, Florida State University College of Business, October 2010.

5 'Maternal employment and child socio-emotional behaviour in the UK: longitudinal evidence from the UK Millennium Cohort Study', Anne McMunn et al., University College London, July 2011, *Journal of Epidemiology & Community Health*, 2011.

6 'Cost of Childcare 2010', Daycare Trust.

7 'Childcare Tax Credit Survey', Netmums & Resolution Foundation, March 2011.

8 Interview in the *Guardian*, 3 July 2010.

9 'Paternal recognition of adult offspring mediated by newly generated CNS neurons', G.K. Mak and S. Weiss, cited by Brian Glossop in *Scientific American*, 17 August 2010.

10 'The maternal brain', Craig Howard Kinsley and Kelly G. Lambert, *Scientific American*, January 2006.

11 'Pup exposure differentially enhances foraging ability in primiparous and nulliparous rats', K.G. Lambet, A.E. Berry, E. Amory, E. Madonia, G. Griffin and C.H. Kinsley, *Physiology & Behaviour*, 2005.

12 'Affective and neuroendocrine correlates of fatherhood in a biparental mammal, the California mouse', M. Chauke, T.R. de Jong, K.R. Measor, B.N. Harris, M. Antonious, and W. Saltzman, paper presented at 'Parental Brain and the Next Generation' Conference, Edinburgh, 2010.

13   'Own baby cry and picture stimuli activate parent brains according to gender, experience, psychology and dyadic relationship', J. Swain, J. Leckman, L. Mayes, R. Feldman, E. Hoyt, H. Kang, P. Kim and R. Schultz 2007.

14   'Fathers have lower salivary testosterone levels than unmarried men and married non-fathers in Beijing, China', Peter B. Gray, Chi-Fu Jeffrey Yang and G. Harrison Pope Jnr, 2006.

15   'Male and Female', Margaret Mead, 1953.

16   *Daily Mail*, 26 October 2010.

17   Analysis by Oriel Sullivan, Centre for Time Use Research, University of Oxford, April 2010.

18   Interview in *Radio Times*, November 2010.

19   Interview in *The Scotsman*, 4 October 2009.

20   'Greater Expectations', Equal Opportunities Commission, 2005.

2. CLOCKING OFF

1   Office of National Statistics, earnings data for April 2010.

2   *21 Hours: Why a Shorter Working Week Can Help Us All To Flourish*, Anna Coote, Andrew Simms and Jane Franklin, New Economics Foundation, 2010.

3   *Working Hours in the Recession*, Chartered Institute of Personnel Development, August 2010.

4   'The part time pay penalty: earning trajectories of British women', M. Connolly and M. Gregory, *Oxford Economic Papers*, Vol. 61, April 2009, p. 76–97.

5   *Daily Mail*, 11 November 2009.

6   See 'Happiness: Lessons from a New Science', Richard Layard, 2005, and *Off-Ramps and On-Ramps: Keeping Talented Women on the Road to Success*, Sylvia Ann Hewlett, 2007.

7   Interview in *The Times*, 21 May 2011.

8   *Journal of Labor Research*, cited in *Men's Health* magazine, April 2011.

9   Chartered Management Institute survey, cited in 'Managers' pay gap widens for first time in decade', article in *Personnel Today*, 11 September 2007.

10   *Off-Ramps and On-Ramps: Keeping Talented Women on the Road to Success*, Sylvia Ann Hewlett, 2007.

11   Cited in *Sunday Telegraph*, 6 August 2011.

3. DADDY WARS

1   Fisher et al., cited in 'Fatherhood Institute Research Summary', January 2011.

2   Eurobarometer poll, 'Gender Equality in the EU 2009'.

3   National maternity survey 2010, Maggie Redshaw and Katriina Heikkila (CORR Katriina Heikkila).

4   *Unlocking the Full Potential of Women in the US Economy*, Joanna Barsh and Loraina Yee, 2011.

5   Interview for CBS *Sixty Minutes*, 14 June 2006.

6   Third Work Life Balance Employee Survey, DTI, 2007.

7   YouGov and Centre for Policy Studies poll, February 2009.

8   'The Intimate Father: Defining Parental Involvement', Esther Dermott, *2003 Sociological Research Online*, Vol. 8 No. 4.

9   Third Work Life Balance Employee Survey, DTI, 2007.

10   In *The Bastard on the Couch*, ed. Daniel Jones, 2004.

11   'Stereotype Threat and Women's Math Performance', Steven J. Spencer, Claude Steele and Diane M. Quinn, *1999 Journal of Experimental Social Psychology*, Vol. 35.

12   'Stereotype Threat Effects on Black and White Athletic

Performance', Jeff Stone, Christian I. Lynch, Mike Sjomelig and John M. Darley, *1999 Journal of Personality and Social Psychology*, December 1999, Vol. 77 (6).

13   'Links between young people's relationships with their fathers and their mothers, and their wellbeing and self-esteem', report published in 2010 by the Fatherhood Commission, body established by the Children's Society.

14   'Parental Investment in Childhood and Educational Qualifications: Can greater parental involvement mediate the effects of socioeconomic disadvantage?', Darcy Hango, *Social Science Research*, Vol. 36, Issue 4, December 2007.

15   'Fatherhood: evolution and human paternal behaviour', Peter B. Gray and Kermyt G. Anderson, Harvard University Press, 2010.

4. FOR BETTER, FOR WORSE

1   *What Moms Think: Career vs Paycheck, Working Mother Magazine* report, 2010.

2   Interview in the *Telegraph*, 2 June 2009.

3   'Marital estrangement, positive affect, and locus of control among spouses of workaholics and spouses of nonworkaholics: a national study', *American Journal of Family Therapy*, B. Robinson, J. Carroll and F. Flowers, 2001.

4   'Squeezed Britain: Low to middle earners audit 2010', report by Matthew Whitaker for Resolution Foundation, November 2010.

5   *The Times*, 20 August 2010.

6   'Gender Equality in the EU in 2009', Eurobarometer poll, 2009.

7   'Men's Unpaid Work and Divorce: Reassessing Specialisation and Trade', Wendy Sigle-Rushton, *Feminist Economics*, April 2010.

8   Office of National Statistics, June 2011.

9   'On the road. Social aspects of commuting long distances to work', Erika Sandow, University of Umea, cited in *Daily Mail*, 26 May 2011.

10   'The Instability of Divorce Risk Factors in the UK', Tak Wing Chan and Brendan Halpin, April 2008, http://users.ox.ac.uk/~sfos0006/papers/change8.pdf.

11   'Household Responsibilities, Income and Ambulatory Blood Pressure Among Working Men and Women', Rebecca C. Thurston, Andrew Sherwood, Karen A. Matthews and James A. Blumenthal, *Psychosomatic Medicine*, February/March 2011, Vol. 73, No. 2.

12   *Flexible Working: Benefits and Barriers*, Government Equalities Office, 2009.

13   The *Observer* magazine, February 2011.

14   'We'll Cost You Some Friends, Mummy', article in *Sunday Times*, 13 June 2010.

15   *Off-Ramps and On-Ramps: Keeping Talented Women on the Road to Success*, Sylvia Ann Hewlett, 2007.

16   Fatherhood Institute research summary, January 2011.

17   Interview in the *Guardian*, 27 September 2010.

18   Suzi Godson, www.moresexdaily.com.

19   Centre for Labour Research at Adelaide University, via the Better Health Channel website, www. betterhealth.vic.gov. au.

20   Cited by Suzi Godson, moresexdaily.com.

21   *Why Marriages Succeed or Fail*, John Gottman, 1994.

22   'An anatomy of economic inequality in the UK', report from National Equality Panel, 2010.

23   *Grazia* magazine 'Women and Work Survey', June 2010.

5. HALF A WIFE

1   *Working Parttime (Not) a Problem?*, ed. Saskia Keuzenkamp, Netherlands Institute of Social Research, 2009.

2   From author's interview with Sarah Jackson (study not published at time of writing).

3   *Flexible Working: Benefits and Barriers*, Government Equalities Office, 2009.

4   'US National longitudinal lesbian family study: psychological adjustment of 17-year-old adolescents', Nanette Gartrell and Henny Bos, in *Pediatrics*, June 2010.

5   'Transitional phase or a new balance? Working and caring by mothers with young children in the Netherlands', Frits van Wel and Trudie Knijn, *Journal of Family Issues*, May 2006, Vol. 27, p. 633–651.

6   'Third Work Life Balance Employee Survey', Department of Trade & Industry, 2007.

7   Ibid.

6. RETHINKING FAMILY LIFE

1   'Gay fathers expanding the possibilities for all of us', S. Schacher, C. Auerbach and L. Silverstein, 2005, *Journal of GLBT Family Studies*, Vol. 1 (3), p. 31–52.

2   *Work Life Balance: Working for Fathers?*, Working Families, 2010.

3   'The chore free teens who never cook, wash or clean', *Daily Mail*, 24 June 2010.

4   Analysis of data from the Child Development Supplement of the Panel Study of Income Dynamics, University of California, Riverside, June 2003.

5   'Rethinking the Family', report from Grandparents Plus, March 2009.

6   *Battle for Female Talent in Emerging Markets*, Sylvia Ann Hewlett and Ripa Rashid, December 2010.

7   Interview, *Sunday Times*, 14 March 2010.

8   'Childcare, eldercare and the labour force participation of married women in urban China 1982–2000', Margaret Maurer-Fazio et al., *Journal of Human Resources*, Vol. 46, 2011, p. 261–294.

9   Annual Grant Thornton International Business Report, March 2009.

10   Grandparents Plus Survey, June 2010.

11   Ibid.

12   Office of National Statistics, Statistical Bulletin: Cohort Fertility 2009, 9 December 2010.

13   Interview, *Sunday Times*, 10 October 2010.

14   Quoted in *Straits Times*, 12 October 2010.

15   UN World Population Prospects Report, 2006.

16   *Daily Mail*, 20 December 2010.

17   From author's interview with Andrew G. Marshall.

18   'Population Trends Summer 2002: Attitudes towards ideal family size of different ethnic/nationality groups in Great Britain, France and Germany', Office of National Statistics, 2002.

19   Social Trends Report, 2007, Office of National Statistics.

20   *Families and Work*, Office of National Statistics, July 2005.

21   Rake et al., 2000, cited in Women and Work Commission, *Shaping a Fairer Future*, 2006.

22   'Family planning and age related reproductive risk', D. Utting and S. Bewley *Obstetrician & Gynaecologist*, 27 January 2011.

23   'A reluctance to embrace the one child family in Britain?', paper prepared for EURESCO conference 'The Second Demographic Transition in Europe', Julie Jefferies, June 2001, Germany.

24   Ibid.

25   'The Only Child: Debunking the Myths', article in *Time* magazine by Lauren Sandler, 8 July 2010, and 'Only Children and Personality Development: A Qualitative Review', Denise F. Polit and Toni Falbo, *Journal of Marriage and Family*, Vol. 49, No. 2, 1987.

26   'Good for nothing? Number of siblings and friendship nominations among adolescents', Donna Bobbitt-Zeher and Douglas B. Downey, cited in *New York Times*, 10 September 2010.

7. THE GLASS ELEVATOR

1   *The Long History of Old Age*, ed. Pat Thane, 2005.

2   Article in *The Guardian*, 22 January 2011, 'Confessions of a Menopausal Mother'.

3   'The Grey Economy: How Third Age Entrepreneurs are contributing to growth', Ron Botham and Andrew Graves report for NESTA (National Endowment for Science and Technology and the Arts), August 2009.

4   Statistical analysis from 'The Employment Rate of Older Workers', Ulrike Hotopp, in Labour Market Trends, February 2005, Office of National Statistics; Labour Market Statistical Bulletin, July 2011 (ONS); and author's analysis of previous ONS statistical bulletins.

5   Women and Work Commission Progress Review, 'Towards a Fairer Future: Implementing the Women and Work Commission Recommendations', April 2007, Department for Communities and Local Government.

6   Interview in *The National*, 27 December 2008.

7   *Unlocking the Full Potential of Women in the US Economy*, Joanna Barsh and Lareina Yee, 2011.

8   'Making talent a strategic priority', Matthew Guthridge, Asmus B. Komm and Emily Lawson, *McKinsey Quarterly*, January 2008.

9   *The New New Inbox*, by Pierre Khawand, 2010.

10   'Meta-analysis: the relationship between engagement at work and organizational outcomes', James K. Harter, Frank L. Schmidt, Emily A. Killham and Sangeeta Agrawal, published by Gallup, 2009.

8. TIME FOR A CHANGE

1   US Air Force website, 31 March 2011.

2   'CBI Employment Trends 2009: Work patterns in the recession', report by Andy Bockless and Mike Noakes for Confederation of British Industry, 2009.

3   'Flexible Working: Working for Families, Working for Business', Report of the Family Friendly Working Hours Taskforce (of which the author was a member), Department for Work and Pensions, 2010.

4   Ibid.

5   *Workshifting Benefits: The Bottom Line*, Kate Lister, Telework Research Network, May 2010.

6   *These Four Walls: The Real British Office*, Gensler, 2005.

7   'Smashing the clock', *Bloomberg Businessweek*, 11 December 2006; 'Reworking work', *Time* magazine, 18 July 2005.

8   Interview, *Daily Telegraph*, 14 August 2010.

9   'Flexible Working', DWP.

10   Women and Work Commission, 2005.

11   *Class of 2010*, Jen Lexmond and William Bradley for Demos, 2010.

12   Department for Businesss, Industry & Skills, press release, 1 June 2011.

13 'Flexible Working', DWP.

14 *HR and Payroll Management Systems*, survey by Conspectus, January 2009.

15 *Third Work Life Balance Employee Survey*, Department of Trade & Industry.

16 *Desperately Seeking Flexibility – Is Job Sharing the Answer?*, Carol Savage, Dr Karen Janman and John Knell, Industrial Society, 2001.

17 BBC World Service interview, 6 October 2008.

18 *Personnel Today*, May 2009.

19 *Quality Part Time Work: A Review of the Evidence*, Clare Lyonette, Beate Balduf and Heike Behle Mar, March 2010.

20 S. Connolly and M. Gregory, 'Moving down: women's part time work and occupational change in Britain 1991–2001', cited in 'Flexible Working', DWP.

21 *'Quality Part-time Work: An Evaluation of the Quality Part-time Work Fund*, Clare Lyonette and Beate Baldauf, November 2010.

9. LINES OF DESIRE

1 *Tackling Housing Market Volatility*, report by the Joseph Rowntree Foundation, May 2011.

2 Ibid.

3 Analysis by Office of National Statistics for the Live/Work Network, 2011.

4 *21 Hours: Why a Shorter Working Week Can Help Us All to Flourish in the 21st Century*, report by Anna Coote, Andrew Simms and Jane Franklin for the New Economics Foundation, February 2010.

5 *Increasing Passenger Rail Capacity*, Commons Public Accounts Committee Report, November 2010.

6   *Bureaucrats or Architects? Recasting the European Welfare State*, Gøsta Esping-Andersen, 2000.

7   *Cost of a Child 2011*, report from insurers LV=.

8   Scottish Widows UK Pension Report, June 2009.

8a   'Childcare and Early Years Survey of parents 2009', research report for Department for Education, 2010.

10   Unpublished Office of National Statistics data cited by Dr Catherine Hakim in *Childless in Europe*, research report for the Economic and Social Research Council (ESRC), 2002.

11   *Employer Best Practices for Workers with Caregiving Responsibilities*, Equal Opportunities Employment Commission, 2009.

INDEX